Media & Kids

REAL-WORLD LEARNING IN THE SCHOOLS

Author Notes

James Morrow's knowledge of media, kids, and the real world goes back to his own ninth-grade filmmaking, an endeavor which garnered him an honorable mention in one of the first Kodak Teenage Movie Contests. He has since worked as a teacher, writer, cartoonist, and movie producer. He is the author of *Moviemaking Illustrated* (with Murray Suid) and he has won a CINE Golden Eagle for his documentary short, *Children of the Morning*.

Murray Suid is a staff writer for *Learning* magazine. He has written *Painting with the Sun* (a first book of photography) and, with Roberta Suid, *Happy Birthday to U.S.* (an activity book on American culture). His short films include *How to Make Home Movies Your Friends Will Want to See Twice* and *The J-Walker*. His first formal training in media production came at the hands of one of his high-school students.

REAL-WORLD LEARNING
IN THE SCHOOLS

Media & Kids

James Morrow
and Murray Suid

HAYDEN BOOK COMPANY, INC.
Rochelle Park, New Jersey

To Richard Jones,
the teacher's teacher,
and to Jean Pierce Morrow,
who works so well with media and kids.

Acknowledgments for Previously Copyrighted Material

Chapter 1: The concept sketches and captions are from *Visual Thinking* by Rudolph Arnheim, © 1969, reprinted by permission of the University of California Press.

Chapter 3: The excerpt on Ralph Chesse's puppetry is from "Conversation with a Puppeteer" by Tim Holt, published in *California Living Magazine,* April 28, 1974. Every reasonable effort has been made to locate the author of this piece, but this has regrettably proved impossible. The "magic act" and the "comedy routine" activities were based in part on material written by Louis Phillips for *K-Eight* Magazine and *Learning* Magazine, respectively.

Chapter 4: The principles of drawing and the drawing lessons are from *Drawing Textbook* by Bruce McIntyre, reprinted by permission of the author. The elephant sketch is from *Children Solve Problems* by Edward De Bono, © 1972, reprinted by permission of Harper & Row. The exploratorium photo is reprinted by permission of *Learning* Magazine.

Chapter 5: The *Science Fiction Horror Movie Pocket Computer* is by Gahan Wilson and is reprinted by permission of the author. The handwritten text is from *Being of the Sun* by Ramon Sender and Alicia Bay Laurel, © 1973, and is reprinted by permission of Harper & Row.

Chapter 9: The photo of rear-screen projection is from *Using Closed-Circuit TV in the Schools* by Shirley L. Marionoff, © 1970, reprinted by permission of the School District of Philadelphia.

Chapter 8: The still from *It Came From Beneath The Sea* is reprinted by permission of A. S. Barnes and Company.

Acknowledgments for Original Photos, Art, and Text

Note: Work by children is credited in the captions found throughout the book.

p. 8, drawing by Ron Harris; p. 25, photo (center) by Bob Mell; p. 25, photo (bottom) by Jean Morrow; p. 32, photo by Jean Morrow; p. 37, photo by Murray Suid; p. 41, photo by Jean Morrow; pp. 46-50, drawings by Ron Harris; p. 55, photo (top) by James Morrow; p. 55, photo (bottom) by Phiz Mezy; pp. 59-61, drawings by Ron Harris, script by James Morrow; p. 80, photos by Eileen Christelow; p. 81, photos by James Morrow; p. 82, photos by Eileen Christelow; p. 83, photos by Eileen Christelow; p. 84, photos by Ron Harris and Eileen Christelow; p. 88, photos by Gretchen Henry and Joseph Henry; p. 89, photo by James Morrow; p. 89, chart by Murray Suid; p. 93, drawings by Ron Harris; p. 100, sound essay by Steve Daniels; p. 102, drawings by Ron Harris; p. 115, photo by Jean Morrow; p. 125, photos by Jean Morrow; p. 128, photos by Jean Morrow.

Library of Congress Cataloging in Publication Data

Morrow, James,   date
  Media & kids.

  Includes index.
    1. Audio-visual education.   2.   Mass media.
  I.   Suid, Murray I., joint author.   II.   Title.
  LB1043.M74   372.1'33   76-39941
  ISBN   0-8104-5798-9

1	2	3	4	5	6	7	8	9	PRINTING
77	78	79	80	81	82	83	84	85	YEAR

Book design by Roberta Suid and Ron Harris

Thanks

It would be impossible to list all of the friends and colleagues who helped us to learn something about media and kids during the past eight years, or even all those who helped directly with a specific sentence or two of the present book. But we must make special mention of the following special people: Joe Adamson, writer and filmmaker, for commenting on the Introductory Essay and the Movies chapter; Elsie Barnard, communications teacher at Chelmsford High School, for helping to edit the Introductory Essay; Linda Barnes, director of Chelmsford High School's drama club, for some valuable additions to the Stage chapter; Betsey Bohl, the Chelmsford Schools Media Supervisor, for general support and enthusiasm; Bob Boynton and Bill Cook of Hayden Book Company, for an abundance of vital touches; Marjorie Farmer, Executive Director of Reading and Language Arts for the School District of Philadelphia, for sponsoring our initial research into the field; Jim Higgins, Luther Randolph, and Rebecca Smith, former media team at Philadelphia's Vaux Junior High School, for showing us the power of multi-media learning in urban schools; David Mallery of the National Association of Independent Schools, for his continual encouragement and warm heart; Frank McCulloch, Morton Malkofsky, and Bob Bryant of *Learning* Magazine, for contributions to material which originally appeared in their pages; Emily Morrow, parent of one of the authors, for numerous new wordings; Jean Morrow, the Chelmsford Schools media production specialist, for reading the entire manuscript and convincing us to take out as many falsehoods as possible; Elizabeth Murray, lifetime inspiration to dozens of language arts teachers, for sharpening the Print chapter; Louis Phillips, stand-up comedian and magician, for insights into Stage; Dave Stone, animator and cartoonist, for perusing the Design chapter; Bonnie Sunstein, media-oriented English teacher, for putting her imprint on Print; Neil Weisbrod, director and editor at Boston's WGBH-TV, for grappling with the Television chapter; and Bob Zeeb, English Coordinator of the Newton Public Schools, for the example of his many curricular innovations.

Preface

This book is for teachers. It aims to bridge the gap
between creativity and the curriculum. But none of
the media activities we present—from the radio
play to the documentary film, the song lyric to the
comic book—was dreamed up expressly for the
schools. Each is used every day by adults in the real
world of our culture. As such, these formats go
beyond one-shot classroom projects to become
vessels which a student can fill repeatedly in his or
her later life. This book is for teachers, but it is also
for fathers, mothers, aunts, uncles, Girl Scout
leaders, daycare directors, school administrators,
education professors, and everyone else concerned
with creativity, communication, or kids.

Contents

Note: °in the text indicates that further information on a book or topic under discussion can be found at the end of the chapter under the heading *Sources and Resources.*

Media & Kids

REAL-WORLD LEARNING IN THE SCHOOLS

Introductory essay
Why the medium is not the message

I

For some educators, "media" is when you show an Encyclopaedia Britannica movie about Canadian fisheries. Thereafter, the definitions range outward to include all non-book learning materials, from sound filmstrips, educational records, overhead transparencies, and super-8mm loops to the more high-powered technology of closed-circuit instructional television, computer terminals, and programmed-learning laboratories.

A few years ago, "media" meant blowing kids' minds with mixed-media shows, featuring the simultaneous presentation of slides, movies, and rock music. Then there's the "media study" movement, an attempt to have students understand the supposed sensory and psychic effects which movies and television exert apart from their content.

Within this diversity of definitions lurk two distinct philosophies of media: 1) Media for the sake of supplementing textbook learning and 2) Media for the sake of media. The first view is readily recognizable as the conventional "audio-visual aids" or "A-V" approach. The second view might be called "Neo-McLuhanism," after its inspiration in the writings of Marshall McLuhan, the famous Canadian communications philosopher to whom we owe the aphorism, "The medium is the message." McLuhan was once a major voice behind the introduction of media study into the curriculum.

My own view, a result of working with media and kids in a variety of school settings over the past eight years, is not so much a synthesis of the A-V and Neo-McLuhanism philosophies as an alternative to them. The vision behind this book is a vision of the classroom as a place where active production in all media is regarded as a natural way to learn. The authors see children solving problems in the arts and sciences not only through reading and writing, but also through producing radio and television shows, making films, staging playlets, designing posters, taking photographs, and creating numerous other real-world artifacts. Further, we see children responding to each other's productions and to productions from the culture at large intelligently and with feeling.

The distinction between the A-V approach and the one explored in this book is apparent: the child who sits passively and presumably soaks up knowledge from other people's learning materials vs. the child who actively conceives, researches, and executes his own learning materials. These student-made learning materials need not be limited to the so-called "instructional media." I believe that no medium is inherently instructional or non-instructional, and that a "popular culture" medium like the comic book can influence a child's growth as positively as a school-endorsed medium like the overhead transparency.

A similar conviction separates this book from Neo-McLuhanism. In the face of much fancy talk to the contrary, I have come to feel that any medium *per se* is really quite neutral. A humanistic approach to media means understanding that human inten-

The ultimate rewards of media production lie in the domain of wit and imagination.

tions, not media themselves, make the messages. If those messages are dull, offensive, dishonest, or repressive, it's not the medium's fault. It's the fault of people.

By extension, I find little to applaud in the Neo-McLuhanistic use of the word "media" to mean primarily new technological media like television and film. In my view, speech is a medium, too. So is print. So are stage, design, and a multitude of subforms that kids have always used for active production (puppet shows, drawings, short stories, dioramas, skits). The significance of twentieth century technology in all this is simply that it increases the variety of media modes, thus maximizing the individual's chances of finding forms that work well for him.

Finally, while Neo-McLuhanism has made itself attractive primarily to teachers of English and art, I believe that media can facilitate learning in all subject areas: science, mathematics, social studies, foreign languages, industrial arts, physical and health education. That is, I feel media production should occur in a classroom's on-going program, and not just in special filmmaking courses, after-school photography clubs, or one-shot communications units.

In my experience, when media becomes a "cause" within a school, and not simply a normal means to particular creative ends, a tendency develops to assume that the best and ultimate media activities are the "pure" ones (drawing on film, pin-hole camera building) that don't relate to anything besides media. This book presumes that the "ultimate" rewards of media production lie in a different domain, the domain of wit and imagination and making contact with people. The exciting thing about most children's films, for example, is not that they are films or that they got made, but that they often contain nutty—or moving—little moments that have an effect on us as an audience.

The chapters that follow explain how media-oriented learning can work in any curriculum. Before turning to these practicalities, however, I would like to review the phenomenon of Neo-McLuhanism and the forms (like "visual literacy") in which this philosophy continues to permeate educational practice. My aim is to clear the air of a few lingering rhe-

torical cobwebs, establish some historical perspectives, and help you to avoid frustrating encounters with slogans, conferences, and degree programs that seem to support the kind of learning explained in this book but end up functioning at cross-purposes to it.

II

The grip of McLuhan's followers on media-in-education was once so powerful that many teachers got the impression that it was not possible even to think about making films or photographs in their classrooms unless they first agreed that "the media" had reorganized kids' nervous systems, that the content of a movie is secondary to whether it is presented on TV or in a theater, that print would be obsolete by 1980, and that electronic circuitry was turning this barrier-ridden world of ours into a "global village" of intimacy and kinship.

For all this, the roots of McLuhanism in American education are actually rather rational. They go back to the growing availability in the late 1950s and early 1960s of 16mm prints of commercial movies for classroom rental. A number of notable educators who loved film soon made the discovery that it was possible to analyze a good movie like *The Hustler* or *On The Waterfront* in a manner analogous to the analysis of a good book. But there was an additional payoff: the students didn't have to do any reading. Kids who couldn't get through books were now able to contribute to the discussion, often quite meaningfully, in a way which demonstrated that illiteracy is not the same thing as stupidity.

Then a great film critic intervened. "If you think movies can't be killed," cautioned Pauline Kael in a famous address, "then you underestimate the power of education." Taking this warning to heart, a large number of movie-minded English teachers started searching for an approach to film that avoided bookishness and focused on the medium's own special properties. They thought they found what they were looking for in Marshall McLuhan, and so began flocking to McLuhan-oriented conferences sponsored by The Center for Communications in New York City (since transmuted into The Center for Understanding Media in homage to McLuhan's most famous book). In 1968 I attended one of these, widely advertised in educational circles as the Sixth Annual Fordham University Film Conference.

The Sixth Annual Fordham University Film Conference was for two kinds of people: teachers and trainers of teachers. The teachers came to be trained. The teacher-trainers came to put on a show. There were lots of flashy films, lots of flashy names (Judith Crist, John Schlesinger, Frank and Eleanor Perry, Marshall McLuhan), and lots of flashy lecturers congratulating each other on being "practicing fanatics," but all anybody got to take back to his classroom was a large metal button that said "Fordham Loves Film."

Film study, that nice, respectable, low-key movement in education, had gotten completely out of hand. One by one, the hard-core McLuhanites at the conference rose to present renditions of an argument that goes something like this (after you finish saying, "as McLuhan has observed"): Today's kids are growing up, with extraordinary depth and involvement, in a unique, non-linear environment defined by the "new electronic media" (meaning television). This environment has endowed them with a set of perceptual predispositions which are quite different from and, truth to tell, "better" than those of their local teachers, parents, and McLuhan experts. These are the children of a "post-literate" society. The teacher who ignores this fact is riding for a fall. There is even a word for such squares. They are called "pobs" ("print-oriented bastards").

From McLuhan, these lecturers had learned the potential of a startling fact. With grim faces and gasps of concern, they read from their innumerable magazine articles how "the average child, when he reaches age 15, will have clocked only 10,800 hours of classroom time as compared with 15,000 hours of TV-watching time." If ever numbers were a call to action, this surely was such a time.

But wait a minute. If TV is already giving kids a full supply of transcendent perceptions, aren't these statistics cause for consolation rather than arousal? Indeed, what other conclusion can we draw but that schools ought to proceed with their traditional emphasis on reading and writing, if only for the sake of preventing kids from growing up with what McLuhan himself would call a "sensory imbalance" (television being weighted, in McLuhan's estimation, against vision and in favor of hearing and touching)? Shouldn't we keep the screen-oriented bastards (s.o.b.'s) and their satchels of TV commercials as far from the curriculum as possible?

McLuhan's reputation had catapulted film study to the forefront of educational innovation, all right, but at a stiff price. The movement's leaders were simply not allowed to answer such questions with rational remarks like, "But you see, most of what kids see on the tube is junk, and we want them to respond critically." No, one must always resist judging the message, because it's the medium that counts, and

the true believer does not go around distinguishing quantity from quality.

McLuhan was saddling his disciples with an absurd, unwieldy, the-customer-is-always-right theory of schooling. "Communicating with kids," especially urban Black kids, "where they're at" (television ads, movies, rock music) quickly became an end in itself. Nobody seemed to know where to go from there or if, indeed, it was even advisable to go anywhere from there. After all, injecting a non-linear child with reading, writing, and other middle class conventions might warp him for life.

The committed educator's ideal continues to be competence, not compensation.

But what teacher starts trying to "communicate" with kids through reading and writing anyway? All the teachers I know *talk* with their students, in the old "oral-aural" mode that McLuhan favors, and it doesn't make much difference whether everybody shares the same pop-culture background or not. As for reading and writing, is it really endorsing WASP values to make a post-literate child literate? Does unfamiliarity with print really mean that the kid is compensated in some mythic, perceptually superior way known only to "practicing fanatics"?

The Noble Savage has made guest appearances in American education before, and every time the long-run, genuinely humanistic response has been to acknowledge his need to make it in an unjust, imperfect, WASP's nest of a world, even if this means corrupting him with literacy. The committed educator's ideal continues to be competence, not compensation. Yet the McLuhanites always seemed to find satisfaction in selling out to kids—to their interests, however directionless, to their tastes, however capricious, to their "perceptions," however wrong.

Some disciples even tried enticing the Noble Savage into the active phase of media study. Filmmaking, which I had always assumed was just about the most technically demanding art ever invented, was suddenly revealed as mere child's play. Only the fainthearted fussed over it. "Young people," wrote a ranking McLuhanite in *Saturday Review*,° "are not afraid to carry a running projector around, spraying the images on walls and ceilings for distortions which communicate." Which communicate what? Chaos?

This same author further probed the Noble Savage's psyche by submitting youth-oriented television to laughable little "studies," all of them carefully designed to prove nothing. "The difference between *Star Trek* and *Mission Impossible* marks the trend toward self-explanatory images that need no dialogue," he reported. "Take an audio-tape of these two popular TV shows, as we did in a recent study, and it will reveal that while *Mission Impossible* is completely unintelligible without images, *Star Trek* is simply an illustrated radio serial, complete on the level of sound."

Some trend. As it turned out, *Mission Impossible* went off the air sooner than *Star Trek*, which survives as of this writing in the form of a Saturday morning cartoon show, highly successful re-runs, and a cult of loyal fans who actually hold conferences of their own. It would seem that content, imagination, and words count for something even with today's allegedly "visual" kids.

III

During all these years of McLuhan's ostensibly happy marriage with film study, a joker lay hidden in the deck. Fordham may have loved film, but Marshall McLuhan did not.

From those early, exciting *On The Waterfront* discussions, the McLuhanites had inherited a commitment to motion pictures as the essential synonym for "media" and, indeed, as the panacea for the now-generation's educational ills. Not only that, they had also inherited a commitment to consider film as a basically emotional, sensory, *visual* experience rather than a narrative or dramatic one.

McLuhan, meanwhile, had decided that vision was selling us down the river of cold, heartless cognition. The problem with print, the most visual of all media (a discovery the visual literacy people have yet to make), was that it overstimulated the eye at the expense of the ear and skin, those parts of the body where McLuhan locates the feelingful, tribal impulses of the human spirit.

Television, not film, was for McLuhan the hope of the future. Here was a truly involving experience, a "cool" medium whose visual bankruptcy required the audience to enter a "tactual-auditory" frame of mind and actively construct its own *gestalt*. Film, on the other hand, was a "hot" medium, of such high image fidelity that nobody got to participate. It would seem that any unprejudiced reading of McLuhan could not help turning up just as many arguments *against* film study as in favor of it!

Foreseeing philosophical disaster, a few of the more quick-witted film study enthusiasts began talking about movies the way McLuhan talked about television. Movies involve "all the senses" someone would announce bi-hourly at the Fordham film conferences, without realizing that the designation applies even better to "old media" like plays, circus acts, and dinner table conversations.

A second line of defense appeared in a *Saturday Review* article celebrating today's "non-linear, unstructured (films) that leave out sequence, motivation, and 'argument'," which was a mighty peculiar way to characterize most of the examples the author gave, such as *Rosemary's Baby, The Graduate*, and *2001: A Space Odyssey*. All of these non-linear, non-literary pictures, as it happens, are based on books. Just off hand, I can't think of a more carefully structured movie than *2001: A Space Odyssey*. And even as a *medium*, film has never been more inherently "non-linear" than print. Indeed, when we read, we often engage in the rather "unstructured" practice of retracing our progress or glancing at footnotes, whereas with a movie there is the unvarying, "linear" experience of scene following scene, shot following shot, frame following frame.

IV

The defense failed, and orthodox McLuhanism strangled on its own cant and self-contradictions. But the basic attitude behind the movement—sensory input as the key to "understanding media"—did not disappear. Rather, it got reassigned to the campaign for something called "visual literacy."

Since printed words are themselves visual images, the term "visual literacy" is on the face of it a less-than-illuminating redundancy. What the movement's leaders really seem to have in mind is not visual literacy but *visuals* literacy, "visuals" being their significant-sounding word for pictures. They want kids, in the words of an Eastman Kodak Corporation pamphlet, to "be able to read visuals as they would read printed matter and . . . write visually using cameras or other suitable devices."

Now that is very nice, but I can't help making the hardly profound observation that people, kids included, do not require exposure to a Kodak curriculum before they can follow the progression of a photo essay, comic book, TV show, or movie. Kids learn how to "read visuals" pretty much the same way they learn how to talk, by sensory exposure, informal parental input, and trial and error. Yet, warns one visual literacy expert, ". . . Film study is as essential as language study. Otherwise, the people will be unable to understand, much less truly appreciate, what they are seeing in theaters and viewing six hours a day on television."

Of all the unwarranted scares to shake our schools, visual illiteracy takes the cake. The reason kids watch films and TV programs is that they *do* understand and appreciate them. The reason many kids don't spend six hours a day reading is that they are not able to understand and appreciate books. You may be sure that the vast commercial enterprises in the land which grind out theatrical films and TV fare are not about to put themselves out of business by suddenly going inscrutable on us.

Of course, children will criticize and interpret the images they decode with varying degrees of sophistication, but then you're no longer questioning their "literacy," any more than you would question the "literacy" of a student who failed to notice *Cinderella*'s theme of "It pays to be beautiful" or the Biblical allegory in Kafka's *The Trial*. Yet the movement's leaders seem perfectly willing to circulate their coinage with all its connotations, so that visual literacy, like "conventional literacy," becomes a fixed state—either you have it or you don't—achievement of which among the general populace is still a lofty ideal.

What we have here is a curious reversal of the the-customer-is-always-right theory of education. Now the customer has problems he doesn't even know about. In my more cynical moments, visual literacy impresses me less as a fundamental human faculty and more as what Madison Avenue calls a "created need," manufactured and peddled to the schools in the interest of its inventors. Convenient, isn't it, that the movement is already set up to put cameras into kids' hands so they can start "writing"? Eastman Kodak Corporation, you might recall, does not make ball bearings.

V

In their more perverse moments, the visual literates can be caught attempting to link their work to recent "findings" in cognitive psychology and transformational grammar. "Now can you see that . . . pictures have subject elements, predicate elements, and object elements just like written sentences?" asks a Kodak filmstrip. To prove the point, the authors take a photograph of a "playful dog" challenging an "angry turtle" and break it into three sub-photographs: one of the dog (subject element), one of the dog's snout in near contact with the turtle's (predicate element), and one of the turtle (object element).

This activity certainly uses pictures as a legitimate aid in teaching about sentences and their parts, but it's a lunatic's theory of the graphic arts. It turns the photograph into a hall of mirrors, for every "subject" sub-photograph itself has subject, predi-cate, and object elements ("the dog has brown eyes") and so on, *ad infinitum*. And while I don't mind snapshots of dogs harassing turtles and children playing with balloons and other fulfillments of Kodak's idea of a photograph being used as aids in grammar instruction, I'd hate to see this approach tried with *good* photographs. Who wants to take that great shot of the Black accordianist playing "Going Home" and weeping over the death of F.D.R. and parse even its *literal* meaning?

There is, to be sure, an important, scientifically justifiable move toward greater understanding and use of the sensory basis of intellect. Much current research indicates that well-organized thinking proceeds directly from well-organized perceptual-motor functioning. But what really seems called for are early childhood education programs that capitalize on all the senses, not just sight, and with the ultimate intention of developing the brain itself, not just peripheral faculties.

It is the brain, after all, where vision really occurs, which is why "visual" media are not automatically any more visual than "non-visual" media like sound or print. A good radio play can conjure up mental images that wildly transcend any conceivable photograph of a dog molesting a turtle. The word "macabre" is more visually provocative than most of the pictures that adorn a typical Kodak visual literacy pamphlet. (The word "macabre" is more interesting to *look at* than most of the pictures that adorn a typical Kodak visual literacy pamphlet.)

What *about* words? Where do they fit in? Most drearily, the visual literates have started to believe all the terribly urgent things they said to get their grant money. "Today we proliferate visual language—symbols, message carriers, body language—on television, in film, and in advertising." The implication is that visual language is essentially a phenomenon of "today." It is not. The visual dimension of communications media is less absolute and more wordbound than ever before in history.

Take the case of advertising. The visual literates love to go on about the "visual language" of contemporary magazine and TV advertisements and how this makes America a "visual culture." Nuts. Almost all ads rely on words to make their point. Without words, the visuals become trivial and ambiguous. The essential dynamic, from the idea conference to the concept itself to the final paste-up, rests on an underpinning of words, not images. To maintain that advertisements—or movies, photo essays, comic books, and television shows, for that matter—have little to do with verbal thinking is to be totally out of touch with the processes by which modern media productions actually get made.

As a matter of fact, you have to go back pretty far to find examples of purely visual salesmanship—to early hieroglyphics, persuading the visually literate Egyptian of his king's fortitude in battle, or at least to Romanesque churches, advertising the unpleasantries of hell with such sculpturesque conviction that few sinners missed the message. Why don't the Neo-McLuhanites just come out and say they don't believe a visual image is a visual image unless a camera made it? Why don't they just come out and say that to bring off their philosophy you have to believe that all the "visual media" were invented last week?

Visual-verbal interdependence in media is certainly not a bad thing (unless, I suppose, companies with vested interests in the primacy of the visual are picking up the tab). Word-image juxtaposition is often precisely what makes communication happen. It may even have a lot to do with why kids seem to find TV, comics, and movies more involving than purely visual media like painting and books.

As with the false dichotomy which the orthodox McLuhanites erected between "old print media" and "new electronic media," the false dichotomy which the visual literates erect between "verbal media" and "visual media" robs them of anything resembling a program. In one of their booklets, the Kodakians assert that "visual literacy is more than putting cameras in children's hands or giving children pictures to arrange in some order," yet, when you look around, doling out cameras to click and pictures to sequence is apparently all that these people *can* think up to do with media in the schools.

The underlying motivation of some visual literates is fairly clear. By talking up the "visual" dimension of media, it is possible for them to do what Theodore Roszak calls gate-crashing the creative life. As long as they can get an image to come out on film or tape, they can be, in their own words, "film artists" and "video artists." But the more distanced the movement becomes from the concerns and struggles of media practitioners in the real world, the more self-serving and riddled with myths it becomes.

Jacques Tourneur, who directed, in association with Val Lewton, some of the more eerily effective B-horror-movies of the Forties, summarized a piece of this reality nicely in a recent interview: "Every time you see a film that you like, somebody stayed up at night, somebody didn't sleep, somebody was fussy. . . . Good pictures don't just happen. If a picture's well-written, the guy worked hard. He didn't just write it off the cuff . . . he worked. If it's the direction, it didn't just happen; somebody worried about it. Val and I . . . were proud of our work."°

That, I think, is a worthy and accurate insight into the demanding, idiosyncratic, uniquely rewarding world of media production, an insight worth bringing into our classrooms and communicating to our students. It has a lot to do with people, only a little to do with the senses, and nothing to do with spraying images on walls.

Sources and Resources

1. The best introduction to McLuhanism is Marshall McLuhan's *Understanding Media* (New York: McGraw-Hill, 1964). The best rebuttal to McLuhanism is Jonathan Miller's *Marshall McLuhan* (New York: Viking Press, 1971). Dr. Miller is both a brain surgeon and a noted actor-writer-director, and is thus in a position to counter McLuhan's "scientific" pronouncements as well as his aesthetic ones.
2. Before he flipped out over television, McLuhan helped edit a fascinating anthology of media readings called *Explorations in Communication* (Boston: Beacon Press, 1960).
3. Indirect arguments against visual literacy training are available in a book edited by Jerome Bruner called *Studies in Cognitive Growth* (New York: John Wiley and Sons, 1966). In the first chapter, Bruner implies that overemphasis on pictorial modes of thought can actually inhibit mental development.
4. The *Saturday Review* quotations come from Anthony Schillaci's article, "Film As Environment" (December 28, 1968).
5. Jacques Tourneur's comments on film directing were published in *Cinefantastique* (Summer, 1973).

A model for multi-media learning 1

We learn by doing. Experiences which actively engage our hands and eyes stay with us. Perhaps the true virtue of modern culture is the rich variety of media it affords for understanding and expressing ideas in the arts and sciences. Movies, radio, design, photography, print, and all the other communication forms are available to us not only as sources of information and pleasure, but as graspable tools for active, creative, and, ultimately, educational production.

Real-world Learning

Traditionally, schools run a poor second to the real world when it comes to letting people learn through media. For example, if you lived through the McCarthy era in American politics (the anti-Communist one, not the anti-war one), you may have learned what was going on through as many as seven distinct media.

You probably debated the McCarthy issue with your friends. Toward the end of the era, you might have seen a production of Arthur Miller's *The Crucible.* (If you're an actor, you might have been in one.) In other words, you learned through the medium of STAGE.

You may have seen pro-McCarthy or anti-Communist posters on the street, or read an anti-Communist comic book. (The authors recall an *Uncle Scrooge* adventure of the Fifties in which a foreign country of seeming Communist rule tries to steal the world's rarest element from the world's richest duck.) In other words, you learned through the medium of DESIGN.

You probably read newspaper and magazine articles about McCarthy. You may have recorded your own reactions and observations in letters to friends. In other words, you learned through the medium of PRINT.

You may have seen reproductions of the famous photograph that the McCarthy forces had doctored before introducing as evidence in the Army-McCarthy hearings. In other words, you learned through the medium of PHOTOGRAPHY.

You probably heard, and heard about, McCarthy on the RADIO.

You probably became aware of a McCarthyistic trend in the MOVIES (overtly in *Night People*, more obliquely in films like *Red Planet Mars* and *Invasion of the Body Snatchers*).

You probably saw some of the Army-McCarthy hearings on TELEVISION.

In more recent years, it is likely that you learned about the second McCarthy era—the Eugene McCarthy anti-war one—through some or all of the seven media identified above. The following experiences may come to mind:

Stage: Watching or taking part in marches; hearing pro-war and anti-war speeches.

Design: Seeing or wearing symbolic designs such as flags, the peace symbol, or military stripes.

Print: Reading newspapers or books about Vietnam; writing letters to the editor or to a friend.

Photography: Looking at photographs such as the Pulitzer-winning shot of the execution of a suspected Viet Cong terrorist by the Saigon Chief of Police.

Radio: Hearing the news, as well as patriotic or protest songs, on the radio.

Movies: Watching movies like *The Green Berets, The Anderson Platoon, Carry It On,* or *The Year of the Pig.*

Television: Watching Presidential press conferences on TV.

If the media of our culture are used so naturally and extensively for learning outside the classroom, why are they not more central to the average school's program? Part of the problem is that teachers do not have any schema for applying real-world learning formats to the curriculum. It is much easier to see how a commercially produced filmstrip called *The Navajo People* might relate to a fourth grade study of Indian life than how "the medium of design" might relate to a fourth grade study of Indian life. Once the breakthrough occurs—once you have seen your kids excitedly involved in making Navajo sand paintings—you are likely to value "the medium of design" more than a dozen prepackaged filmstrips with curriculum-oriented titles. But without a model that organizes all basic media into some simple, easily recalled pattern, it is difficult for teachers to think up appropriate activities and connect them to authentic learning goals.

The Family of Media

One model of multi-media learning that has been used with success by teachers and curriculum planners is called the Wheel. We begin with the hub: whatever topic, theme, concept, or content area is under consideration. Around this hub are placed the seven distinct media or "media groups" already discussed.

Stage: Gesture, Speech, Movement.

Design: Drawing, Graphics, Painting, Sculpture, Architecture, Crafts.

Print: Written Words, Numbers, Symbols, and Signs such as $, ?, &, Ω, =, and ‡.

Photography: Prints, Slides (transparencies), Halftone Reproductions.

Radio: Recorded Music, Sound Effects, Dramatic and Comedic Dialogue, and all the other dimensions of sound which radio helped define.

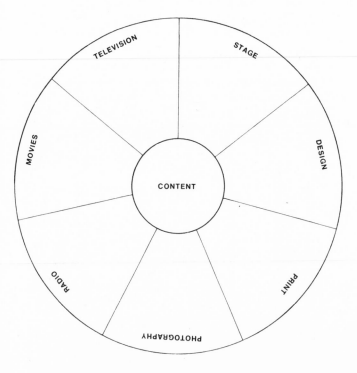

The Wheel: a model for multi-media learning.

Movies: Sound and Silent, Animated and Live-action.

Television: Broadcast and Closed-circuit, Live and Videotaped.

The circular design of the Wheel is intended to convey the overlapping, cyclic quality of real-world learning. In finding out about the fight against cancer, for example, most of us don't say, "First I ought to read a good magazine article about the problem, then I'll go to a lecture about it, then I'll observe a Jimmy Fund poster, then I'll catch the NBC special on television." Rather, learning experiences occur spontaneously, informally, and redundantly.

This is not to imply that multi-media learning in schools requires no planning or organization on the teacher's part. It merely means that each medium is to be valued for its own special properties, its own integrity, and that no one form is *ipso facto* better than any other. Ideally, the decision to use a film rather than a book or to make a slide-tape rather than a film is never based on favoritism or financial commitment, but on pedagogy. Depending on the problem, only one medium may be the "right" one for the job. Thus, even if your school has invested heavily in a television studio, a film collection, or an art room, there still will be occasions when you pass over these impressive installations in favor of a modest slide show or a written assignment. Each medium deserves, and has been given, an equal segment of the Wheel.

Another advantage of using a circular model is the suggestion that each medium has the potential to interact with and enrich the others. Note how adjacent media in particular have a tendency to pair off. Our culture affords many instances of the union of stage and design: protest marches, circuses, formal drama. Design, print, and photography fuse in myriad forms: posters, advertisements, newspapers, magazines, books, comic books. (In Europe, comics often use photographs instead of drawings.)

Radio and movies at first seem an unlikely combination, but in 1925 there was a plan afoot, reported in *Motion Picture Magazine*, to broadcast the voices of movie actors into theaters playing their films. (It never got off the ground.) Eventually, the world of sound, as radio had helped define and refine it, was able to be recorded on cylinders, discs, film, and tape, thus permitting the kind of "soundtrack" used in movies and, more recently, slide-tapes.

Movies and television are combined all the time. Nightly news programs rely on film clips for on-the-spot reporting, and children's shows often alternate studio production with cartoons. Movie directors

sometimes develop a character by showing how he or she reacts (or fails to react) to TV images, as in *Save The Tiger, Seven Days In May, Persona,* and *Targets.*

Coming full cycle, it is easy to see how television interacts with the medium of stage, both in public broadcasts (sports events, ballets, ventriloquism acts) and in closed-circuit "feedback" (therapy situations, athletic training, theater rehearsals).

The position of each medium on our model reflects not only "media interaction," but also "media evolution." Starting with stage and moving clockwise, the Wheel gives a simplified picture of the history of communication.

Stage was the first medium—even animals engage in play. Next came design, as demonstrated by the prehistoric paintings in the caverns of Altamira in Spain. Print, in the sense of written language, was by definition the first historic medium. Compared with these first three media, the electrochemical half of the Wheel has developed almost instantaneously and simultaneously, but it is still possible to chart the progression from photography to radio to the unifying of sight and sound in movies and television. (Radio and the movies paralleled each other most closely—the public began seeing movies around 1896, which was also the year of the first significant "wireless" demonstration.)

Our more McLuhanized educators like to believe that the history of communication is a continuing saga of new media eclipsing the old. (That is why when they talk about "the media," they usually mean only recent technological forms—photography, radio, movies, and television; often they really mean only television.) Examples of this unfounded, survival-of-the-fittest theory are a whole chapter in the history of self-interested prophecy.

When movies firmly established themselves as an art form in the 1920s, academicians lined up to say last rites for the theater. Yet if you decide you want to see a play this week, you probably won't have much trouble finding one. Photography was going to make painting obsolete. Artists still paint. Movies were never going to survive television. They have.

The media can use each other to define themselves and grow.

The vitality of media holds no matter how far back you go in history. The emergence of print from the design medium (hieroglyphics and pictograms), for example, did not stop people from drawing pictures, even though print was generally a much more efficient way to present ideas. Of course, certain subforms of a basic medium may disappear over the years, but the loss is never total.

Thus, you no longer find many people, even monks, doing illuminated manuscripts, but the basic idea is alive and well in picture books and comic books. Similarly, while magic lantern slides are antiques, the generic medium, the "transparency" (the 35mm slide, the overhead projectual), is still very much with us.

From humanity's first meaningful grimace to the latest computer graphics, the evidence supports the idea that the family of media is harmonious, and grows stronger with the arrival of each new member. This is really a three-stage process. In the first stage, the new medium appears on the scene and borrows heavily from one or more older media. In the second stage, it asserts its independence from other forms and explores its own unique potential. At the same time, the new medium inevitably suggests unexpected possibilities in an older one. In the third stage, the necessity to defend the older medium against the new no longer seems so crucial. Experiments with "pure form," while still exciting and rewarding, are no longer viewed as the only way to rescue the medium from extinction. Conventional practice is again legitimized.

The relationship between *photography* and *design* (most especially painting) offers a clear example of this process. It is sometimes forgotten today that pioneering photographers were strongly influenced by painting in selecting subjects for their cameras. The early history of photography is replete with shots of nudes posing awkwardly while shutter times elapse and bunches of fruit sitting around in brass goblets waiting to be turned into still lifes—quaint relics of a time when the larger possibilities of the medium simply hadn't occurred to anyone. Then came the second stage, with photographers going out into the streets, freezing moments of historic importance and making unhistoric moments seem important because they were frozen. Meanwhile, painters were responding to the new medium, exploring, through Impressionism, those elements that were unique to their art: color, the surface of the canvas, paint itself. Stage three is now with us. We again value the representational element in painting (Andrew Wyeth, Norman Rockwell), and we value the paintings of the past more than ever, and on their own terms. Photography, for all its "photographic detail," still finds itself hard put to match the vibrant, transcendent naturalism of a Flemish Early-Renaissance masterpiece.

Print, too, has functioned as both catalyst and beneficiary of media evolution. Stage, film, and television all enriched print by adding their various script formats to the range of writing genres. Prose style itself has been influenced by other media: the "pictorial" detail of Dickens, the "photographic" naturalism of Frank Norris and Upton Sinclair, the "cinematic" stream-of-consciousness of James Joyce. Meanwhile, it's worth remembering that without print, coherent organizing of ideas for films, TV shows, and radio programs would border on the impossible.

When *holography* (three-dimensional laser photography) finally gets going it, too, will probably follow this pattern, having the same sort of invigorating impact on photography that photography had on painting. When moving holograms are invented, they will no doubt challenge—and then vitalize—movies and television. And so it goes. The point is that media are continually evolving because of their dynamic interdependence. Not only can we use all the media to heighten our powers of expression, but the media can use each other to define themselves and grow.

Real-world Learning in the Schools

When employing the Wheel model in curriculum building and classroom teaching, it is important to realize that every communications medium has two "poles" or "phases." In the *active* phase, the communicator produces a message—he *gestures* or *says something* or *makes a photograph* or *writes a poem*. In the *reactive* phase, the communicator receives a message—he *hears a song* or *reads a story* or *views a film*—and tries to make something of it.

There is nothing passive about reacting. If you've ever tried to watch a movie, read a book, or listen to a speech while you are tired or distracted, you know the importance of energy and concentration in message-receiving. Likewise, you can appreciate the amount of experience, desire, and skill that reacting can involve by comparing a novice's critical responses with those of an expert.

We believe learning includes the same two phases. The teacher, thus, has the twin responsibilities of helping students learn how to create their own messages in response to authentic curricular problems and how to react in meaningful ways.

This is where the Wheel comes in. Think of it as the framework of any curriculum unit. Under each medium on the rim, you can write in *materials* (books, films, and other software) and *activities* (production projects) that confront the content being studied. We call this "creating a Wheel," though the process actually calls for creating two Wheels: a Presentation-Wheel which leads to reacting and a Production-Wheel which leads to active problem-solving and creation.

When we speak of students reacting to a Presentation-Wheel, we don't mean that the teacher will read a poem or show a film and then give a test on the symbolism to find out if the class got it. A more authentic model of reacting, based on learning in the real world, begins with the simple (re)act of "enjoying" or "disliking" the work. (Too often in schools, this important decision is passed over; whatever the teacher serves must be "good.") The next stage is informal discussion—a free, possibly passionate give-and-take in which primary reactions clash and illuminate one another. This sort of reacting occurs when adults go to a coffee shop and fight about the movie they have just seen, or when kids debate the latest pop-music hit with their parents. Finally, there is the reacting that professional critics do—formal, solidified judgments about artistry and truthfulness. To achieve this level, students should read works by professional critics, a task quite different from studying the "thought questions" at the end of the chapter.

Beyond aesthetics, reacting includes absorbing what the work has to teach. A world history instructor who decides to present D.W. Griffith's film, *Orphans of the Storm*, for example, will probably want students to go beyond the initial discussion of whether the work is successful *as a film* to consider how accurately Griffith informs us about the French Revolution.

This same concern with concrete learning is at the heart of what we mean by active problem-solving. The rationale of a Production-Wheel is not simply that students should become involved in a lot of different media projects. When Suzie shows us her new 8mm movie about snails, we are concerned not only with how exciting and assured the show is, but also with how much knowledge about snails Suzie gained

from making it and her classmates gained from viewing it.

Even the teacher can learn from a student's production. For example, the authors recently saw a slide-tape by a group of ninth graders about the Cuban Missile Crisis. Technically, the show was not outstanding, but we found ourselves impressed by the simple fact that we, as people who had pretty much forgotten about the Cuban Missile Crisis, picked up a great deal of discussion-provoking information on the subject.

Here is an example of the entire process of creating a Wheel. Suppose a high school English class is dealing with the concept of "dreams." Using the Wheel, the teacher and students begin to plan reactive experiences. Under each medium, they write in particular materials, both real-world and "educational," that can be located easily and brought into the classroom. The same procedure is followed when the class plans the active phase of learning. The sample Production-Wheel on the next page contains five problems which the student solves by making media artifacts.

As this example reveals, it's not enough to know that the medium of "photography" exists or that "radio" may have great potential in the classroom. Communicators must be able to go beyond general

No matter what the curriculum topic, the Wheel can help you.

categories and work within specific formats. These are covered in the *Activities* sections of chapters three through nine. In the Design chapter, for example, we discuss *the illustration*, *the one-panel cartoon*, *the comic book*, *the poster*, *the diagram*, *the diorama*, *the exploratorium*, and *the board game*.

The range of content that can be covered through this approach is as vast as all of culture. The Wheel, after all, is based on real-world learning, which encompasses the physical sciences, the social sciences, technology, and the arts. No matter what the curriculum topic of the hour, the Wheel can help you and your students organize learning experiences.

For instance, if a science class is studying insects, each student might do all or part of his own Insect Wheel. In the active phase, he could: pantomine an

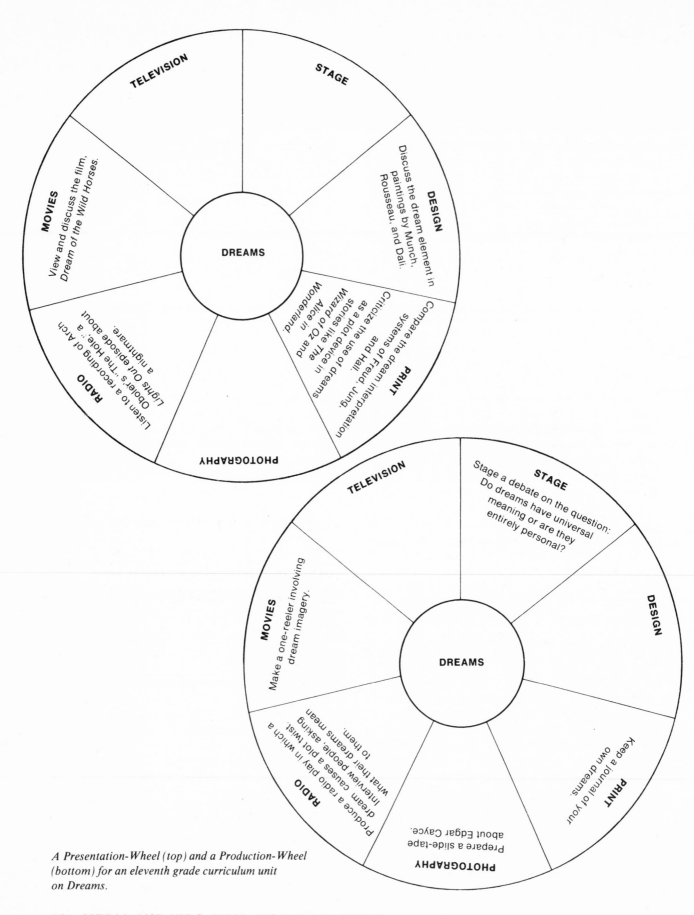

A Presentation-Wheel (top) and a Production-Wheel (bottom) for an eleventh grade curriculum unit on Dreams.

inchworm (stage medium), construct an insect diorama (design medium), write a short story about insects taking over the world (print medium), make a slide-tape juxtaposing bug spray advertisements with pictures showing how insects benefit humanity (photography medium), and produce a ten-minute videotape on how to make a caterpillar zoo (television medium).

The appendix of this book contains three more Presentation-Wheels and three more Production-Wheels. We tried to choose samples that would demonstrate how multi-media learning can be applied to the full range of grade levels. Thus, we have a fourth grade Wheel (on Law), a seventh grade Wheel (on The Short Story), and an eleventh grade Wheel (on Time).

In a Wheel-oriented curriculum, the teacher sometimes sets up both the presentations and the projects. Other times, the students do the Wheel-making, either individually or in groups. The goal, we think, is for the learning to be student-centered. Depending on the grade level of the class and the experience of the teacher, the trend would be for the student to choose a topic which has meaning to him and the media he'll use to explore it. The teacher would function increasingly as consultant and resource person.

This philosophy helps avoid a common pitfall of curriculum planning: teacher-generated problems which seem intriguing on the surface but which are so specific they do not allow for personal, varied invention by the child. For example, a "radio" activity we once concocted asks the student to role-play a baseball announcer, substituting new, colorful terms for the basic clichés. The catch is that most kids cannot think of anything very interesting or witty to say —they are unable to take the idea anywhere. The problem is more clever than any solution to it could be.

Because of the boom in commercially produced "A-V software," the creation of Presentation-Wheels is an easy task in most subject areas. Unfortunately, this often leads curriculum planners to neglect the active, project-oriented phase of learning. In this, they are simply reflecting the bias of the culture at large, in which most of us spend more time reading or watching TV than we do working on home movies, writing stories, or creating our own greeting cards.

Some very real dangers lurk in this bias. If "media" as an educational force is defined primarily in terms of exciting kids with "multi-sensory materials," then the implicit lesson becomes that instant

Most of us spend more time reading or watching TV than we do working on home movies or writing stories.

"Equality among individuals."

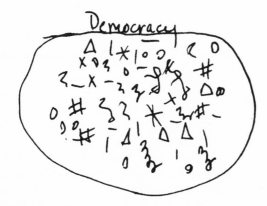

"All types can fit into system (outer circle) in harmony and without losing their identity . . . All contribute to the whole."

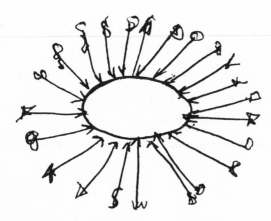

"Everyone free to take part in government. Great differences in background."

Drawing out an idea: students in a visual thinking experiment used pictures and words to clarify their "views" of democracy.

gratification and immediate apprehension are always good. Yet, experiments have shown that without some kind of mutual reinforcement between brain and body, as opposed to passive "sensory stimulation," learning will be stifled and learning ability itself will be inadequately developed.

In the late sixties, Professor Rudolph Arnheim of Harvard directed a project in which subjects were asked simply to take a piece of paper and make abstract drawings of various concepts, such as democracy, youth, good marriage, and bad marriage.° Several examples appear on this page. Take a minute to try it yourself, drawing the concept "freedom."

You probably discovered, as Arnheim's subjects did, that this kind of problem-solving is not simply a matter of copying some fixed image out of your head. Rather, you had to think through and clarify, or even discover, your own personal idea of freedom. Conscious activity helped you to learn.

In most schools, kids learn actively in two media only: *print* and *stage*. Schools do expect students to write and give oral reports. Arnheim's experiment suggests that *design*, too, should be included in the active phase of classroom learning. We view this book as an attempt to expand Arnheim's theory by showing how "learning through conscious activity" can occur in *all* the media outlined on the Wheel.

Limitations of the Model

The Wheel is only one of many possible frameworks for multiplying learning options for children.° Those who disagree with our particular arrangement, or who feel that the seven-segment schema presented here contains too many or too few media, are invited to create their own version. The important thing is to come up with a model that makes sense to the teacher and students who will be using it.

A potential drawback of any schema is that it will be followed too rigidly. The Wheel is a model, not a mandate. There is no requirement that every medium be used every time. In theory, of course, the more forms that come into play, the more opportunities for the child to learn the content. (Students who think they know all about the idea under consideration after a single production or presentation may be surprised by the new perspectives that come from working through the same problem in another medium.) But if the student has truly caught on, don't drive the issue into the ground just because the Wheel says it's time to make a movie about it. The Wheel was not designed to create multi-media boredom.

Ultimately, then, the Wheel is something like a blank lesson plan. Some teachers and students will want to work it out on paper. Others will simply carry it around in their heads. Many educators who have never seen anything as formal as the Wheel use this kind of multi-media approach intuitively when guiding their classes.

A second potential drawback of the model is that it seems not only to expect too much of the individual teacher, but to require a school system wired to the rafters with every conceivable form of electronic gimmickry. At first glance, no one short of a combination Mr. Fix-It and Renaissance Man is competent to teach the Wheel. Each segment could easily be the stuff of a whole course's study, a whole life's study, and throwing them all together might appear nothing short of perverse.

In practice, things are a lot simpler. "Creating a Wheel" usually means creating a mini-Wheel, a version of the model tailored to the needs, resources, and skills of the given teacher, students, and school. For example, one basic kind of Wheel activity, developed by a media team at Vaux Junior High School in Philadelphia, engaged students in picking a topic of personal interest, such as clothing style or popular music; writing a list of twenty-five things they considered important about that topic (print medium); using that list to focus their thinking while writing a story, play, poem, or essay about the topic (print medium); recording their writing on tape (radio medium); making a list of photographs that would complement the tape (print medium); signing out an Instamatic camera and taking slides suggested on the list (photography medium); and, finally, selecting, arranging, and timing the slides to synchronize with the tape. While the end product was a slide-tape

rather than a complete Wheel, students came at the subject in a way that emphasized the educational value of three distinct media and the power of interacting them.

A project like this doesn't require incredible teacher-training or exotic equipment. Most teachers can handle simple still cameras and tape recorders. Most schools have such tools available. Or teachers can borrow them from friends or students. The software—film, processing, tapes—for the Vaux slide-tapes came to less than $2.50 per student. (Many kids worked in groups.)

The rest of this book describes each of the particular media which comprise the Wheel. These chapters focus on media rather than on messages simply because we assume that you as a teacher already *know* many potential contents for kids' productions—the various curriculum topics you are developing in your daily work. What you may not know is how your students can begin to put these topics into the form of an animated cartoon, slide-tape, puppet show, sound essay, or poster.

Our media chapters aim to give you the nuts and bolts of such production by defining the medium at hand, outlining the *concepts* (conventions, grammar, concerns, principles) which both professionals and amateurs must know to use the medium effectively, suggesting classroom production *activities*, and presenting *standards* by which kids may evaluate and improve their work. Before leaping into such particulars, though, we want to share our tentative answers to some pedagogical questions that teachers ask when trying to harness media.

Sources and Resources

1. Rudolph Arnheim's experiment is written up in his remarkable book, *Visual Thinking* (Berkeley and Los Angeles: University of California Press, 1969). Further activities along these lines are available in a wonderful workbook by Robert H. McKim called *Experiences in Visual Thinking* (Monterey, CA: Brooks/Cole Publishing Company, 1972). The reader is reminded that visual *thinking* is a quite different concept from visual *literacy*. As McKim puts it, "To believe that seeing is merely a matter of turning on the senses, and not also turning on the intellect and the unique human capacity to elicit imagery with words, is to miss a crucial point" (p. 62-63).
2. Two classic accounts of a "multi-media" or "Wheel" approach to formal education are Douglas

Lowndes's *Film Making in Schools* (New York: Watson-Guptill Publications, 1968) and Elwyn Richardson's *In the Early World: Discovering Art through Crafts* (New York: Pantheon Books, 1964). Despite its title, Lowndes's book describes a highly pluralistic curriculum, including simple but imaginative projects in stage, design, photography, radio, and, of course, film. These ideas were developed in England, which is apparently far ahead of America in discovering realistic, diversified uses of media in education. Richardson's book, too, comes to us from outside the United States. It tells about a school in New Zealand where a single learning problem is commonly explored through many different channels, including stage, design, and print.

The pedagogical questions 2

There is nothing quite like the sense of purpose, fun, and real education found "behind the scenes" on a student media production. Movie sets can be especially inspiring—kids bustling about, going over the script, practicing camera movements, aligning lights, adjusting costumes. Everyone is involved.

Unfortunately, the opposite atmosphere also happens. In one corner, we see some peripheral students threatening to convene a paper airplane derby, pouring Diet Pepsi into the wastebasket, and otherwise conveying the impression that they don't care to be regarded as peripheral. In another corner, two students are fighting over possession of the camera, and it looks as if the camera is going to lose. In the middle of the room, the picture's lead actress is quietly telling you that she plans to be in the hospital for the rest of the month. And, of course, the bell is about to ring, destroying all hope of getting a good "Take 2" to replace the miserable "Take 1" that just transpired. In short, the needs and promises of the production itself have become a mere distraction from the realities of the hour, intruding to the forefront of everyone's thoughts only by accident.

While the ideas in this chapter will not enable you to raise the health level of student performers or rewire the bell system in your school, they should show how you can solve certain media production realities through sound pedagogy. Armed with this knowledge, you will have an easier time coping with those obstacles to real-world learning over which you have no control.

Literacy

Most schools regard learning as a matter of reading, writing, and sometimes talking. The regular subjects—English, science, social studies, math—are less often *done* than *read about*. This may be dull for kids who can read. For those who can't, it's a nightmare.

A frightening proportion of our students, especially in urban schools, are severely retarded in their literacy, reading several grade levels behind the norm. (Even the notion of reading at a particular grade level is misleading, for a seventh grader reading at a fourth grade level is not reading like a healthy fourth grader, with a sense of growth and joy.) A teaching-learning system that depends primarily on print takes knowledge that is not necessarily beyond a poor reader's intellectual grasp and ruthlessly places it there. Students who fail in reading and writing are not just failing a subject; they are failing their school's chosen mode of communication, and the contents of *all* their various courses are subsequently denied to them.

Media can help these kids be learners in school. Time and again, students who bring a long tradition of personal failure with print into the classroom show themselves able to achieve in the other media.

This does not, of course, relieve us of the obligation to teach print skills—it merely questions the school's wisdom in making learning *contingent* upon print skills. We have no patience with visionary mediacs who feel that the presence of reading and writing in the curriculum bespeaks an outdated definition of learning. It ought to be clear from Chapter 1's account of media evolution that the advent of modern communications technology makes having a handle on print more important than ever. Print is the "wild card medium," underlying not only most other media but nearly every kind of cultural, educational, and vocational fulfillment. Even the so-called non-print occupations (in broadcasting, photography, the crafts) are almost invariably practiced by people who know how to read and write with competence and control. Whether we like it or not, students are judged by their society, their schools, and themselves according to print standards, and getting a job, any job, depends in large measure upon literacy.

The multi-media approach does not deny any of these facts about print, but it does provide a more realistic context for approaching this medium in school. When kids come to see print as just one octave of the media spectrum, they should feel freer to

---

No one ever learned how to read just from making a film.

---

work on both verbal and nonverbal problems. Meanwhile, the fact that they can perceive, communicate, and learn is constantly reinforced for them by their successes in the "non-print" forms.

Such experiences can provide kids who previously had little respect for their own potential not only with a sense of satisfaction, but also with gains in the verbal area. Composing and recording words for a radio drama or a film help many students improve their writing and speaking abilities. Less is known about the effect of multi-media learning on reading, but students certainly acquire needed confidence and pleasure in this skill when they observe themselves in a videotaped reading of a play, or when they read the narration for their slide-tapes into the microphone. Of course, print skills must continue to be taught explicitly; no one ever learned how to read just from making a film.

The whole messy issue of print's place in multimedia education can be summarized as follows: Learning is not strictly a matter of reading and writing. But reading and writing are not strictly a matter of reading and writing either. In the media-oriented school, teachers and students find themselves moving through a variety of modes, at times banging away directly at print skills, at times using expression in other media to improve reading and writing, at times using reading and writing to improve expression in other media.

The world we are heading into requires new competence in old communications skills, as well as in the emerging electrochemical forms. Today's children must learn to use their real eyes and ears and brains if they are truly to understand the TV-eye, the radio-ear, the IBM-brain. To be present and future masters they must be past masters.

Product

In recent years, it has become the fashion among some media teachers to put down "product" in favor of "process" as the goal of classroom media experiences. It doesn't really matter what a kid's film looks like, they say, or even if it exists at all, because the process of working with a camera leads inexorably to a boosted self-image and heightened powers of perception.

Nonsense, we say. Without a commitment to the concept of "product," its sister concept, "production," becomes a sterile abstraction. Unless your students have a real idea in their heads, something that will work as a show and make sense to an audience, their interest in film or radio or TV will not survive the initial "turn on" value of the technology.

When a kid produces a really memorable radio play or film or comedy act or poster series, you may be sure that the "process" he went through was meaningful and rewarding. When a kid produces junk, you may be almost as sure that the process he went through was equally junky.

What we are essentially arguing here is the primacy of *substance* over *form* in media production. Schools often reverse this priority. The student essay which contains a last paragraph beginning "In conclusion," lots of transition words like "nevertheless" and "consequently," and topic sentences that stand out on the page like blood on snow is likely to receive a high mark. That the essay says nothing, that it has no substance, it is not regarded as cause for alarm.

The same phenomenon occurs with "non-print" media. We have known student films featuring razzle-dazzle technique—a zoom to a close-up every two seconds—to be praised over much better efforts displaying no particular preoccupation with form. Media specialists have learned to call the first sort of movie "cinematic," which is supposed to mean it's good.°

This is not to imply that devices like zooms in film and topic sentences in writing are not important, or that technical flaws (non-agreement of subject and verb in writing, poor focus in photography) do not interfere with substance. Technical flaws always interfere with substance, and technical virtuosity can enrich substance immeasurably. Indeed, one purpose of the chapters that follow is to help you and your students learn the formal elements of all the basic media.

But the substance should come first. Sometimes the internal logic of the substance dictates a need for special techniques, in which case the film, photograph, novel, play, or whatever would be impoverished if the communicator did not have them at his command. At other times, the substance suggests a straight-forward, "obvious" approach. A brilliantly funny comedy routine by a student, for example, is generally most effective if the student simply sits on a stool and rattles it off. The effect will only be diminished if he spends half the time mugging or guffawing. Charlie Chaplin put it another way: "If what you're doing is funny, don't be funny doing it." Technical antics do not come across as good use of form, but as obligatory use of form. They turn form into formula.

Planning

Nearly all the real-world movies, radio programs, stage plays, and comic books worth experiencing began life as prose statements. The need for on-paper planning in classroom production is equally crucial. Without some kind of script or outline in hand, it is impossible to evaluate a kid's media production idea before film, time, or other valuable resources are expended on it. Indeed, without some kind of script or outline in hand, it is difficult to be sure the kid really has an idea.

Don't give students a camera with blank film in it or a videotape recorder with blank tape on it simply because they profess a desire to "practice." More likely, they want to hack around. The more chance they get to hack around, the more contempt they will acquire for the medium, and the less motivated they will be to do anything substantive with it. To be sure, students can't produce their scripts unless they know the necessary tools, and a certain amount of unplanned play is desirable. But when the hardware and software are expensive, familiarity should be acquired under teacher supervision. Many kids, you will find, do not know as much about media hardware as they think they know.

Some educators favor "practice exercises"°—giving students little problems to solve using the camera or microphone. If this excites you, by all means try it. In our experience, however, the payoff of practice exercises is limited. Media production in the real world does not get started by doing exercises. It gets started by hitting on ideas for projects. Unless your students have invested time and enthusiasm in good, workable ideas, it won't make any difference whether they've solved practice problems or not. Once they do have ideas, it is usually sufficient to explain to them, slowly and deliberately, how the camera or the microphone or the felt-pen works. They'll pay attention to you, because they'll have reasons to know.

The main issue in media production planning, then, is not whether it should be done, but what format to use. Some common approaches are:

1. A statement of intent. ("This sound essay will document the noises of Fisherman's Wharf between the hours of . . .")
2. A list of shots. ("For my slide-tape about how railroad yards work, I will take a slide of the switch tower, a slide of the block signal, a slide of a diesel switcher, a slide of . . .")
3. An outline of the plot. ("Chapter 1—Introduction of Jamie and his grandparents. Chapter 2—Jamie's watch is stolen and he decides to . . .")
4. A prose description of the action. ("In this comic book, Chameleon-Man foils a band of evil pearl divers by turning blue and . . .")
5. A set of pre-production sketches.
6. A storyboard (pre-production sketches with captions).
7. A complete script.

The decision to use one format rather than another should be based on the nature of the project being planned. Complex, intricately plotted films, for instance, usually require full shooting scripts, while a "cut-out animation" short can easily rest on a simple prose rendition of the story and a few pre-production sketches. This may seem obvious, but it's surprising how readily some educators become committed to particular planning formats in the abstract.

An example is the popular obsession with storyboards. We have met educators who regard storyboards as the only way to plan films, slide-tapes, and TV shows. This is ironic, since in the real world storyboards are often concocted for purely economic or political reasons, as a way to show prospective sponsors how the finished production is going to look, how the special effects can be done cheaply, or how the product's twenty priceless virtues have all been worked in. In our experience, it is common for kids either to expend so much energy producing a storyboard that they lose enthusiasm for the show itself, or to become so wedded to it they lose inspiration and spontaneity on the set.

A similar pitfall can occur with outlining a short story, play, or comic book. Any writer who really

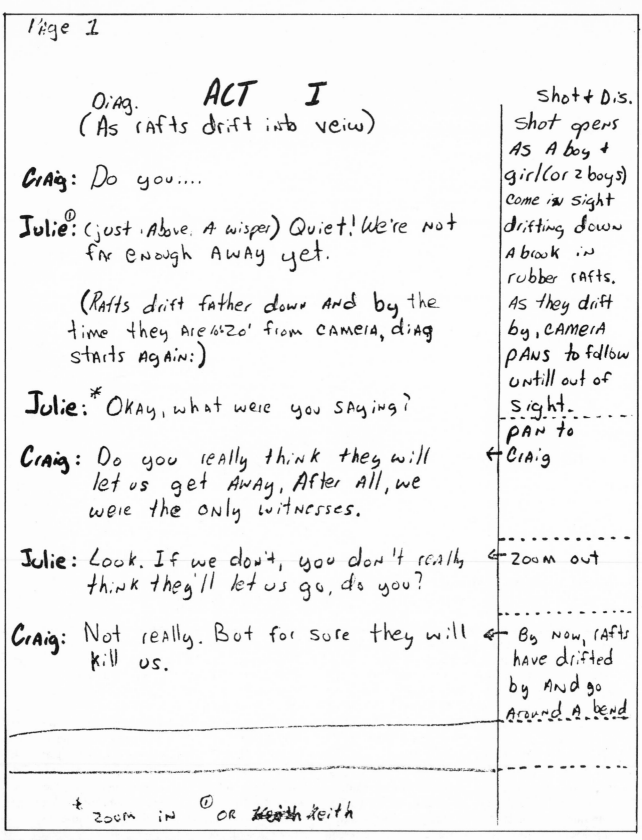

Page 1

Diag. **ACT I**
(As rafts drift into veiw)

Craig: Do you....

Julie[1]: (just above a wisper) Quiet! We're not far enough away yet.

(Rafts drift father down and by the time they are 10-20' from camera, diag starts again:)

Julie:* Okay, what were you saying?

Craig: Do you really think they will let us get away, After all, we were the only witnesses.

Julie: Look. If we don't, you don't really think they'll let us go, do you?

Craig: Not really. But for sure they will kill us.

Shot + Dis.

Shot opens as a boy + girl (or 2 boys) come in sight drifting down a brook in rubber rafts. As they drift by, camera pans to fdlow untill out of sight.

pan to Craig ←

zoom out ←

By now, rafts have drifted by and go around a bend ←

* zoom in [1] or K̶e̶i̶t̶h̶ keith

Television script excerpt by Bill Hood, age 15. Rigid formating and neat typing are not essential to media production planning. Here, "diag." means "dialogue." Camera directions appear on the right.

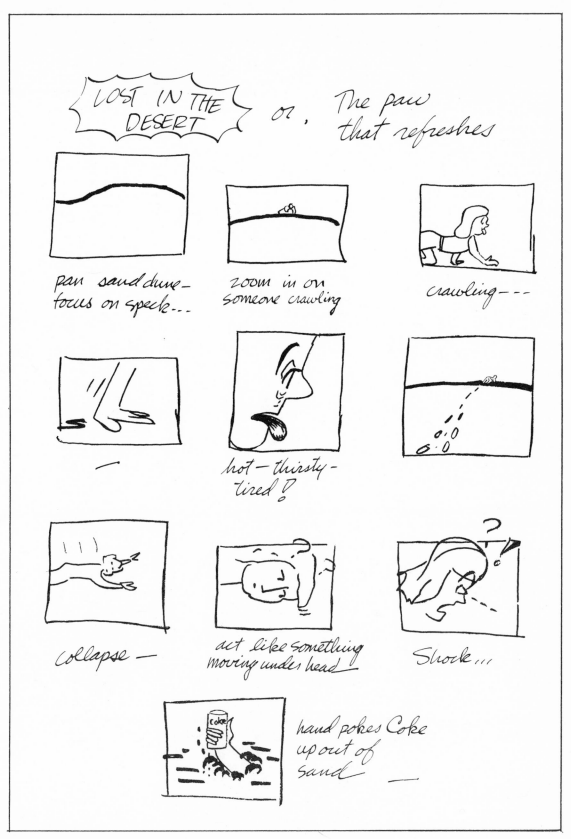

Storyboard by Ron Laird, teacher at the Wyoming School for the Deaf. The sketches were for a film shot by and featuring elementary school children.

knows where he wants his plot to go will intuitively seize upon a kind of free-form outlining. But demands for something called "an outline," complete with lower case letters under arabic numerals under upper case letters under roman numerals, can easily intimidate and discourage the novice writer.

Environment

Sound essays, person-on-the-street interviews, documentary slide-tapes, and similar "on location" projects give kids an opportunity to work in the community at large. But the majority of media activities will still have to be done back at your school. This is unfortunate. There probably isn't a living room in the country that doesn't make a better recording studio, movie set, writer's den, or screening room than the average American classroom.

Problem one is your building's probable preoccupation with windows. The media-oriented teacher has to take a dim view of all this light. Not only will films and slides never reach full potential in any room less than pitch-black, but darkness is often the best environment for hearing a story or an "old radio" tape.

Another problem with many classrooms is sound reverberation, an inevitable characteristic of box-shaped, oversized rooms. Such acoustics can mar the tape recordings students will produce for their radio projects, TV shows, and movies. And, of course, any media show with a soundtrack, whether professional or student-made, carries poorly when presented in an inherently noisy space.

Although teachers have little say in the architectural design of their rooms, they can still transform them with lamps, chairs, rugs, and other goods from home. This possibility is often overlooked, or actively resisted as unorthodox. It's ironic how we rarely hesitate to buy something like a cheap garage-sale chair for our homes, yet don't consider getting one for the environment in which we spend just as many of our waking, productive hours. Assuming the principal is agreeable, consider installing the following items:

Room Dividers and Screens. Some teachers split their rooms into two parts, one "soft," the other "hard." In the hard section, kids sit at their desks, face the blackboard, hear lectures, take exams, and see overhead transparencies. In the soft area, they write, read, record tapes, watch films, and have discussions.

Window Shutters. To block unwanted daylight from your room, hang blankets, curtains, or removable shutters made of heavy "tri-wall" cardboard.

Don't force kids who can't stand each other to work together.

Blankets have the added advantage of absorbing noise.

Platform with Curtain Behind. Not essential, but a boon to all kinds of stage and television activities.

Couches, Rugs, Floor Lamps, Lounging Chairs. These help create the soft area and make good props for many stage, film, and television activities. Also, rugs and cushy furniture reduce unwanted sound reverberation.

Involvement

It is extremely difficult to involve every single student in the production of a class newspaper, movie, slide-tape, or play. Sometimes, of course, kids learn by sitting and watching other kids do things. But in order to give everyone in the class a chance to be productive, we advise the following strategies.

Start with the message, not the medium. An assignment like "Now we're going to make a film" or "Each of you must turn in a comic book" can easily alienate those members of the class who don't care for comics or films and probably never will. Rather, define the problem first: to learn about the Middle East, to understand the planets, to criticize a book, to present your autobiography, to tell a story, to document a place or an event. Each student should then choose which medium he will solve it in and whether he will work on his own or as a member of a group. This increases involvement and shortens the waiting list for particular pieces of equipment.

The issue of grouping deserves special mention. Because media projects frequently require team work, they are good occasions for students to associate with peers of different backgrounds or viewpoints. But this philosophy can be pursued to a fault. Don't force kids who can't stand each other to work together. In real-world media production, antagonistic personalities rarely collaborate if they can help it. One solution is for the teacher to make up groups on the basis of confidential papers submitted by each student listing people he or she would rather not team up with.

The more the teacher is involved, the more the class will be involved. While nothing is quite so pa-

It's all right for the class artist to step in and save a failing comic book or theater set.

thetic as the "class play" in which the teacher writes the show, sews the costumes, and paints the scenery, it is also a mistake to be so fearful of "taking over" that you shy away from demonstrating skills you have that your kids do not. When students come to you with a script they want realized, there's nothing wrong with your actually operating the tape recorder (if it's a radio play) or the still camera (if it's a slide-tape). We have observed class filmmaking projects in which the teacher ran the camera in conjunction with student apprentices, thus guaranteeing that the product would have basic grammatical coherence. But it was still the kids' movie—they wrote it, directed it, determined almost everything that would go up on the screen. Through observation, the apprentices eventually learned most of what the teacher knew about cinematography, and then they took over this function as well.

Use real-world vocabulary. Even the peripheral students at a filming, recording, or acting session will be more cooperative if they feel they are witnessing something real and professional. "Quiet on the set" gets better results than "Could everyone please stop talking now?" "Let's do a Take 2" is preferable to "Well, you really blew it, so now we have to do it again." Sometimes students will take themselves more seriously as actors if during rehearsals you call them by the names of the characters they are playing instead of by their real names.

Encourage students to capitalize on each other's talents. Some educators argue that success in media production is not related to talent. Behind this debatable idea is the truth that, even though someone does not demonstrate an enormous gift for drawing or writing or acting, he should still try these things (and try getting better at them). But the kid who can make startling sound effects with her voice should definitely be singled out and made available to other kids' radio plays. Similarly, it's all right for the class artist to step in and save a failing comic book or theater set, for the class storyteller to suggest a plot for another student's animated cartoon, or for the class musician to add a background score to someone else's movie soundtrack or stage performance.

Authority

We advocate what might be called the "law firm model" of schooling. The teacher is the senior partner, engaged in the same effort and solving the same problems as the juniors. This means you shouldn't ask students to do any media activity, whether it is as complex as making a movie or as straightforward as writing a letter to the editor, that you have not tried on your own.

Without an active "senior partner" in the room, kids may even wonder whether the idea of learning through creative production should be taken seriously or whether it's a gimmick. If you personally have no familiarity with a given form, try calling in one of your school's indigenous media experts—a photographer, filmmaker, sound engineer, or writer whose secret identity may be hidden behind the more respectable role of science teacher, music specialist, custodian, or vice-principal. But in the long run, plan to experience each kind of media production firsthand. Only then will you be able to replace authoritarian comments like "Your plot makes no sense" with authoritative comments like "When I did my slide-tape, nobody could follow it until I added that title about the cream cheese, and I think you have the same sort of problem here."

Readiness

What age "must" a child be before he or she can use cameras intelligently? What drama experiences are "always" meaningful to a fourth grader? These are treacherous questions because individual growth is so much a function of individual endowment and history. The outline that follows is not a set of answers but of observations. Take it as a springboard for deciding what will work in your class.

Kindergarten and Grade 1

Stage: Improvising playlets and skits in front of other class members.

Design: Drawing greeting cards, illustrations for original stories, and one-panel cartoons.

Print: Dictating or writing simple stories, poems, and plays.

Photography: Performing or drawing images for the camera (and speaking for the microphone) in a slide-tape production—equipment operated by teacher or older children.

Radio: Making up and voicing stories—tape recorder operated by teacher or older children.

Movies: Making up and acting out movie stories—camera operated by teacher or older children.

Television: Making up and acting out playlets and skits—equipment operated by teacher or older children.

Grades 2 and 3

Stage: Performing magic shows, comedy routines, speeches, and other planned productions.

Design: Creating simple comic strips, posters, diagrams, and exploratoriums.

Print: Writing simple stories, poems, and plays.

Photography: Producing complete slide-tapes (scripting, visual making, and soundtrack creating)—equipment operated by teacher or older children.

Radio: Producing complete radio dramas (scripting, sound effects making, and acting)—class members operating simple tape recorders.

Movies: Producing live-action movies (scripting, acting, and making sets, costumes, and props)—teacher or older children running camera. Producing animated cartoons (creating artwork for cut-out animation and models for table-top animation)—teacher or older children setting up the camera and class members clicking off the frames.

Television: Producing simple plays in a studio—teacher or older children operating the equipment. Aiming the camera and staging the action in portable video production.

Grades 4, 5, and 6

Stage: Memorizing, rehearsing, and performing a formal play.

Design: Creating comic books that run to several pages, posters that consciously propagandize, and diagrams that solve real problems.

Print: Writing stories and plays running to several pages, poems of several verses, and reviews of books and movies.

Photography: Producing slide-tapes, photo exhibits, and photo essays—class members operating simple "Instamatic" cameras.

Radio: Producing radio dramas—class members operating tape recorder. Producing sound essays outdoors with battery-run machines.

Movies: Producing live-action movies—class members operating simple "Instamatic" cameras. Producing sophisticated cut-out or table-top animation films—teacher or older children setting up the camera and class members clicking off the frames and checking out the shots.

Television: Producing portable video shows—class members operating the equipment under teacher supervision (studio equipment, other than cameras, still operated by teacher or older children).

Grades 7, 8, and 9

Stage: Producing full-length plays, presenting sustained improvisations, and making speeches before large groups.

Design: Greater sophistication and scope to activities already mentioned.

Print: Greater sophistication and scope to activities already mentioned.

Photography: Producing slide-tapes—35mm photography and soundtrack mixing (music under voice) by class members. Creating photo exhibits and essays with 35mm prints.

Radio: Producing full-length radio dramas, including sound effects and music backgrounds—class members doing the recording and mixing.

Movies: Producing live-action and animated movies—class members running the camera and teacher checking out shots occasionally.

Television: Producing studio and portable shows—class members operating all the equipment under teacher supervision.

Grades 10, 11, and 12

A few students really take off. They write novels and plays, produce hour specials for television, and make lengthy 8mm movies. For the average student, you should work toward increasing sophistication and higher standards in the productions suggested thus far: skits, routines, acts, greeting cards, comic books, posters, diagrams, exploratoriums, stories, poems, plays, reviews, scripts, photo exhibits, photo essays, slide-tapes, radio plays, sound essays, live-action films, animated films, portable-television programs, and studio-television programs.

Creativity

All teachers have seen works by children—comic books, TV commercials, stories—that were clearly made in imitation of similar works by adults or even by other children. While our first impulse may be to condemn copying, it is useful to consider this process in the context of other types of expression. Copying and imitation can be thought of as the first steps on a continuum of creative development.

We have devised a model consisting of five levels of increasing originality: copying, imitation, parody, influenced originality, and uniqueness. To clarify the definition of each level, we offer examples from two particular media forms popular among school children—comic strips and still photography. (Keep in mind that the model attempts to reveal something about the growth of kids; it is not necessarily helpful in understanding the real-world artistic output of adults.)

Level 1—Copying. At the first level, the child simply observes someone else's work and duplicates it. He takes a "Peanuts" strip and traces it or reproduces it line for line, or he uses a copy stand to transfer a magazine picture to the slide format.

Level 2—Imitation. At the second level, the child does not have the original work in front of him, and he supplements his recollections with new bits and pieces. But the basic ideas, characters, gestures, plots, gags are still not his own. The child reworks one of Charles Schulz's accounts of Snoopy battling the Red Baron, or snaps his version of a famous photograph.

Level 3—Parody. At this level, the child still takes the basic elements from another source, but he makes fun of them. This is a transitional stage. The child is not full enough of his own ideas to want to try them out, but he is also uncomfortable using other people's ideas as they stand. The Peanuts gang starts to worry about sex, and a photo-advertisement pushing cigarettes finds itself rearranged to emphasize the Surgeon General's warning.

An activity that often occurs at this level is not so much a matter of parodying a known work as paying it homage. Some students are so adept at taking the established conventions and characters from a particular comic book, TV show, or old radio serial and adding their own plots or gags that the results far transcend Level 2-like imitation.

Level 4—Influenced Originality. At the fourth level, the student makes up most of the basic elements, although an immediate source or two of direct inspiration is readily apparent. He draws "Peanuts"-like strips with "Peanuts"-like characters, or he shoots Karsh-like family portraits, but he can legitimately call the productions his own.

An activity that often occurs at this level is "adaptation" or "translation," in which the student takes a story from one medium and tells it in another. For example, when one of the authors was in tenth grade he made an 8mm film of Coleridge's poem, *The Rime of the Ancient Mariner.*

Certain kinds of "satire" are also common at Level 4. Here the student makes fun not of a particular work, as in parody, but of a general media

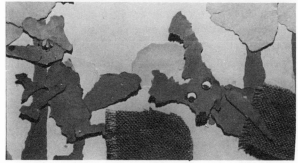

Sending up Peanuts *(top): excerpt from a comic strip by Jack Crivello, age 15 (level 3 creativity).*

In homage to Star Trek *(center): television production by students of Chelmsford High School in Massachusetts (level 3 creativity).*

Adapting Uncle Remus (bottom): artwork used in fifth graders' movie of a Br'er Rabbit story (level 4 creativity).

Under the influence of Poe: excerpt from a short story by Arlene Randall, age 14 (level 4 creativity).

genre. One example we recently saw was an eleventh-grade television production which satirized the spy movie cycle of the sixties.

Level 5—Uniqueness. At the last level, the student is not being guided by a single influence, but by a multiplicity of thoughts, impressions, and feelings gained through his experiences with life and art. The more sophisticated sorts of satire emerge at this level, as well as unmistakable personal style. In drawing a comic strip, making a photograph, or producing any other media artifact, the student is motivated primarily by his own ideas and by his imaginings of the reaction those ideas will elicit from an audience.

Admittedly, no work is completely unique, and every artist acknowledges conscious and unconscious influences. At Level 5, the student may even have one or two particular works in mind, but he uses them mostly for emotional reinforcement. That is, he may want his comic strips to have the same effect that "Peanuts" does or his pictures to have the impact of Eisenstadt, but he does not want them to be *like* "Peanuts" or Eisenstadt.

We call this a model of "creative development," but don't get us wrong. If the development of a child's ability to solve problems with imagination and artistry proceeds through fixed and empirical stages—and this is a dubious idea—then we don't know what they are. When devising an educational theory, there is always a danger of confusing biological growth periods with cultural conventions. It is important, therefore, to understand that this model represents a hierarchy of critical values, not a hierarchy of predetermined steps through which every student will or should pass. In our culture, uniqueness is valued over copying. Assuming the teacher shares this value, the model can be a helpful tool in moving *the child's art* through discrete, increasingly more original levels. There is no evidence to suggest it is meaningful to speak of moving *the child* through these levels.

The ultimate value of the model, then, lies in generating productive classroom discussion and broadening your students' range of creative experiences. Let's say you notice that a kid is always producing imitations (Level 2). You might suggest that, for a change of pace, he or she try twisting the borrowed ideas into humorous effects not intended by their creator (Level 3). And if humor appeals to the child, the next assignment might be to make sport not of a single production but of a general category of production, like pulp fiction, horror movies, soap opera, or musical comedy (Level 4). On the other hand, if a student has invented some wild new comic book hero (Level 5) but is dissatisfied with his art work, it might be worth his time to actually copy a few well-drawn professional strips (Level 1).

Technology

Many teachers have no trouble coordinating media-oriented learning with all the needs discussed so far—literacy, product, planning, environment, involvement, authority, readiness, creativity—yet when it comes to the technology involved they would rather be in Philadelphia. Everything from multiple-camera television to super-8 film loops throws them for a loop.

If you are one of these teachers, let us assure you on the outset that you are absolutely right. Despite what hardware salesmen may tell you, a medium is defined by its grammar, not by the latest technology, and no machine is your friend. The quantity of chintzy, unreliable, perverse, badly-designed equipment unloaded annually on unwary school systems borders on a scandal.

In doing battle with their school's media hardware, many teachers have found wisdom in the following postulates:

1. If your school's A-V specialist has read the operating instructions for a particular machine, that may be the only reason he or she knows more about it than you do.

2. If the hardware malfunctions after you have bothered to familiarize yourself with it, the problem is probably not in you.

3. If the hardware requires a bulb, a filter key, a set of batteries, a three-pronged adapter, a spindle adapter, a power cord, an extension cord, an extension speaker, a microphone, or a pick-up reel, keep an extra of each such accessory in your lower left hand drawer and another in your lower right hand drawer. There are even cases on file in which teachers have not regretted keeping an exact duplicate of the machine of the hour waiting in the wings to back them up.

4. Sex-role stereotyping is as wasteful in relation to media technology as it is in relation to everything else. Don't assume that only the little boys in the class will be interested in running the tape recorder or carrying the tripod. Don't assume that a woman teacher who did not grow up playing around with machines will never acquire facility with classroom hardware. If you can drive a car, maintain a fish tank, run a washing machine, or operate a pencil sharpener, you can learn how to use most media equipment.

A medium is defined by its grammar, not by the latest technology, and no machine is your friend.

At the opposite pole from the A-V salesman's line is the pseudo-humanist's line which goes that it is anti-people, materialistic, and a waste of time to worry about hardware since creativity is a matter of the soul. Don't believe it. You *must* be concerned about hardware if you are going to include a full range of media activities in your curriculum. All machines are not created equal, and anyone who wields a media budget should first do some research.

Above all, we urge you to eschew the "black box" mentality. Super-8 film cartridges, audio-cassettes, video-cassettes, auto-load and auto-thread movie projectors—these are all black boxes. By locking their workings from view and frustrating even the most rudimentary manual intervention, these devices feed the fallacy that technology should be beyond the control of the individual. The black box mentality equates "automatic" and "inaccessible" with "good." It turns tools into machines.

True, for teachers who prefer to know nothing about technology, the attractiveness of black boxes cannot be denied. Teachers who prefer to know nothing about technology, however, have no business trying to make technology pay off, and by embracing all those mummified tapes and films, they play into the hands of people who would play them for fools. But once teachers observe a costly video-cassette or two snarled by an ornery recorder, or a twenty-five dollar super-8 film devoured without apparent motive by a loop projector, then they begin to understand that the price of convenience is at best money and at worst heartache.

Taping the original (as opposed to a duplicate) soundtrack of an important slide-tape on a cassette rather than an open reel is an act of touching but wholly misplaced faith. Spending many hours on a super-8 movie and then packaging the original in a loop cartridge is a folly beyond redemption. Using video-cassettes as the format for master recordings rather than copies of irreplaceable TV shows is a guarantee that Catastrophe will cancel all his plans for the evening.

It is terribly naive to believe that the distributors of 16mm films to schools are indifferent to the outcome of competition between the manufacturers of black box projectors and the manufacturers of manual-loading, gentle-on-film projectors. It is just as naive not to recognize that the professional media magazines which hype the black boxes in so-called "articles" are totally dependent for survival on the advertising of the very companies that make the black boxes. Yet a sizeable proportion of the teaching profession has been brainwashed into believing not only that cassettes and loops have "replaced" open reels, but that they are "better" than open reels!

Cassettes and loops are not better. They are merely convenient. As far as fidelity goes, the average super-8 loop image doesn't look one whit crisper than its open reel counterpart, and the average cassette tape recorder generally sounds several whits worse. We can only be thankful that the literacy problems in this country have not been compounded by the invention of a cassette book.

Audience

Your kids deserve an audience. The expectation of how others will react to a media production constitutes a major motive for going through with it. The actual reaction of an audience—their laughter, tears, or snores—constitutes a basis for reworking or deleting parts of the "finished" product. True, there are many pleasures in solving the internal problems of a production and watching the work of your own hands take tangible form. But in addition we want our words read and our shows shown.

The issue, then, is not whether to provide your students with an audience, but how large to make it. If the audience is too small (say, just you), the producer may feel cheated and wonder why he or she worked so hard. If the audience is too large (say, the whole school or all the participants at a regional conference), everyone may end up feeling a little embarrassed. In general, media productions by kids do not have a great deal of audience appeal beyond the immediate school or classroom in which they were created. But the best judges of which audience to play for are often the students themselves.

The concept of audience can extend beyond the immediate present. It's sad when a kid invests hours of energy in a comic book or slide-tape only to have it misplaced and forgotten by the end of the year. Happily, most teachers take a more respectful attitude, particularly when the production might benefit students in other classes. Assuming the child doesn't want to take the work home right away, the teacher can borrow it and have it catalogued by the school's Instructional Materials Center. Then it can be stored in the A-V closet or even out on a library shelf, alongside the professionally-made learning materials. (Whenever possible, you should circulate a copy of the work, not the original.)

Noise

A subtle but dynamic force resides at the heart of many people's unconscious definition of education, a force which can stop multi-media learning before it starts. On the surface, the problem may be termed "noise." We have witnessed teachers coming down hard on students who were laughing in response to a hilarious scene in a movie. Typically, the film is stopped and the children warned that the program will be cut short if the laughter continues. School teachers and administrators seem to worry a lot about this kind of noise. But we think there is more here than meets the ear.

One of the authors witnessed the following scene in a school for the deaf. The children were lined up outside the cafeteria, waiting to enter for lunch. Nothing much was happening so two third graders began talking to each other in sign language. The person in charge suddenly grabbed both kids and pushed them against a wall. Then she silently rocked an imaginary baby in her arms while glaring at them. Even the naive observer got the message—the boys were out of order because they were doing something different from everybody else; they were, in fact, like babies.

Traditional schools seem intent on maintaining monolithic group behavior. It's all-together-now as we walk down the hall, read the same history text, interpret the same poem, learn the same math theorem. Even programmed instruction courses, which promise individualized learning, inevitably move all the students toward the same ultimate behavior, generally through the same exercises. This is why a single test will suffice to show how well each individual is doing. But authentic learning doesn't come in such neat packages. In the real world, learning splays outward in every direction.

Can school education be as free and open? It will take more than physically open spaces in which everyone goes through the same workbooks. It will take open educators who give students the same rich diversity of materials to react to and create with that the culture at large provides it citizens.

Can schools be open enough to accept classroom productions which are frankly hot to handle? We've seen a student film, made from advertisements clipped out of leading home magazines, that shocked and outraged a group of principals. These administrators were so scandalized by the movie's sexiness that they missed the irony—the images all came from respected journals. Perhaps this is a bizarre example. Probably the film shouldn't have been shown to that audience. Maybe the teacher was an extrovert who wanted to throw some business to the American Civil Liberties Union. But the fact remains: When people (students included) engage in real-life creative efforts or when they are invited to respond to artistic works according to their honest

Can schools be open enough to accept classroom productions which are frankly hot to handle?

Controversial cover for magazine published by the Afro-American Studies class at the Cambridge Pilot School. Art by Barry Langford, age 15.

feelings, the results will not be monolithic, predictable, generally approved of, or necessarily "nice."

Can the same schools that are charged with getting children ready for life be filled with life? This is the pedagogical question that only teachers can answer.

Sources and Resources

1. In a long essay called "Is There a Cure for Film Criticism?" Pauline Kael discusses the pitfalls of insisting that a movie be "cinematic" and missing deeper qualities like imagination, talent, and human revelation. This piece appears in her book, *I Lost It at the Movies* (New York: Bantam Books, 1966).

2. An excellent source for practice exercises is *Doing the Media*, a "portfolio" published by The Center for Understanding Media, 75 Horatio Street, New York, N.Y. 10014.

The medium of stage encompasses an enormous variety of performers: singers, actors, dancers, trapeze artists, magicians, orators, beggars, tour guides, toast masters, clowns, ice capaders, puppeteers, jugglers, auctioneers, ballerinas, stand-up comedians, and sermon-givers. All these people share something that makes them unique among media communicators—they appear live, in person, before those who receive their messages.

Perhaps this "being there for real" is what makes stage so glamorous, so romantic, and causes it to attract a society's most accomplished, graceful, eye-appealing, limber, and poised individuals. Yet, paradoxically, stage is also the medium closest to everyday reality. Its elements—gesture, facial expression, speech, costume—are used by all of us in our daily lives.

Like real stage players, we are often "on"—showing off, playing roles, putting on acts. We tell jokes to amuse our friends. We sing for ourselves in the shower. We stage parties. At dinner time, we dramatize incidents from work, even to the point of imitating the boss's voice to show what dumb thing he said and how we answered it (or should have answered it). Even a four-year-old trying to explain what happened at nursery school will spontaneously leap to center stage kitchen and act out how Melissa boinked Brian.

Concepts

It is unfortunate that this ancient, honored, and accessible medium is so rarely employed in classroom teaching. Stage concepts are familiar and easy to control. The formats are numerous, and most cost little or nothing to produce. The curricular applications are practically without limit.

But even more exciting, we think, is the relevance of stage to the central content of education—the child. For stage, more than any other medium, is about the human condition. Stage offers the best opportunity for students to find out what their bodies can do: the voice, the hand, the glance, the smile. It gives them a chance to explore from the inside out what it might be like to be someone or something else. It even allows children to experiment with emotions like anger and sadness without getting hurt.

Act

"Act" refers to the material someone performs on a stage. In the real world, performers put much time and consideration not only into perfecting a particular comedy routine or set of magic tricks or interpretation of Ibsen, but also into choosing such acts in the first place.

The same principle applies to the classroom. Too often teachers simply hand kids material to perform —a song, a skit, a dance—without realizing how dependent successful stagery can be on a "good fit" between the act and the performer's own style, taste, and personality. The teacher should always try to match the material to the student, which often means letting the student himself make the selection.

Persona

Whatever his act, a performer must render and project a *persona*—a character or personality which may be his natural one but is more often a conscious creation. For example, we know two magicians, one whose character is the rather standard mystic-in-top-hat-and-tails and another who has adopted the more unusual persona of a mute medieval jester.

A crucial component of any stage persona is how the actor looks: his body type, posture, gait, age, hair style, skin coloring, and clothing. How the actor sounds—the speed, accent, and timbre of his voice—is also part of his character. It's even conceivable, in certain kinds of live theater, that smell could be important to a performer's image.

In each case, opportunities for artistic control abound. Through "casting," a theater director can select actors of desired build and type. Hair can be cut, dyed, or augmented with wigs. The body can be costumed. The face can be masked or altered just as radically through make-up.

Even more important than a performer's persona is what he or she does.

Action

Even more important than a performer's persona is what he or she does. In the creation of convincing stage moments, behavior comes before anything else.

Early in his career, the great Russian director Constantin Stanislavsky held that an actor must first of all "feel" angry if he is going to seem angry on the stage or "feel" loyal before he can become a loyal character. Later, Stanislavsky recognized the importance of "doing" anger and "doing" loyalty. The feelings would follow.

For example, if you ask someone to *be* afraid, you will probably get the most stereotyped sort of bug-eyed mugging. But if you simply tell him to *behave* as if you were coming at him with a knife, thus inspiring him to the action of running across the room and accidently knocking over a chair, he will himself start to feel as if he is afraid, and he will come across to the audience as truly afraid.

Professional theater people refer to small bits of stage action as "business" and to full, gross movements as "blocking." In the case of a character who is supposed to be very loyal—to his best friend, say—the "blocking" might require him to subtly but constantly walk in circles around his friend, darting glances outward, as if he were somehow protecting him.

More modest actions can be equally revealing. Hanging up clothes, turning on lamps, jotting down notes, putting on gloves, eating, pouring drinks, coughing, knitting, scratching, playing with one's hair, looking at one's watch, filing one's fingernails, picking up magazines, starting to dial the phone and then deciding otherwise—these are all examples of the sort of "business" actors and directors must constantly invent.

Ideally, business and blocking always grow out of the characterizations and situations, and are never imposed on a scene. Besides increasing the realism and visual intricacy of a play, such actions can serve to lessen a student actor's stage fright by giving him something on which to focus his attention.

The concepts of business and blocking are not limited to conventional play production. All the activities in this chapter—oral narratives, puppet shows, improvisations, magic acts—can profit from the introduction of meaningful, purposeful actions. In a magic act, for example, a bit of intriguing business that catches our attention at just the right time can enable the magician to pull off a sleight-of-hand completely unnoticed.

Space

The word *stage* literally means "standing place." Staging any act is largely a matter of creating a special space for the performer.

Virtually all the paraphernalia associated with stage—curtains, backdrops, platforms, lights—serve to define the performer's area. Within this space, the performer must play his role. Outside it, offstage, he can be himself. It is important, however, to provide the actor with a hidden space, the "wings" of the theater, in which he can mentally work up the transition into his role prior to stepping on stage.

Staging also includes the process of arranging performers about the playing area in a manner that is dramatically efficient (so one player doesn't hide another from the view of the audience) and visually pleasing. When blocking a play, theater directors employ the geographic designations shown at the right.

Thus, directions which an actor typically receives and must interpret include:

"Enter from Stage Left."
"Cross from Center Stage to Up Stage Right."
"Cross from Down Stage Right to Center Stage Left."

None of this means that to stage an act you need a Broadway-type theater. Not many years ago, a group of professional beggars presented their "act" on an underground, moving stage—the New York subway. They moved up and down the aisles, touching the audience (in three senses of the word). They made exits and entrances from either end of the car or, when the police arrived, through the center doors.

Center Stage: the central or middle area of the stage.
Stage Left: the far side of the stage to the *actor's* left when he is standing on the stage facing the audience.
Stage Right: the far side of the stage to the *actor's* right when he is standing on the stage facing the audience.
Up Stage: away from the audience.
Down Stage: toward the audience.
Enter: to come onto the stage.
Exit: to leave the stage.
Cross: to move from one area of the stage to another.

Closer to home, the average classroom also has great stage potential if one is willing to push the furniture around, neutralize the bulletin board with large sheets of solid-color paper, use a wide work table for a speaker's platform, and so on. Cloakrooms, hallways, even playgrounds and swimming pools can be converted into stages. Creating and controlling theatrical environments is well within the manipulative skills of children. This point is clear to anyone who has watched kids at home turning the attic into a fun house or throwing a couple of chairs and an old blanket together to make a puppet stage. To twist Shakespeare: All the world's a stage if you work to make it so.

Audience

The wonderful illusion of stage is that while it generally appears that the actors are directing their behavior only toward each other, they are in fact directing it toward the audience. At the same time, the audience sends back messages telling the performers how they are doing. Audience feedback can take many forms: applauding, laughing, muttering, coughing, being silent, throwing gold coins on the stage, leaving the theater. Positive or negative, it is vital for the performer. When the audience ceases responding, the performer, in show business parlance, *dies*.

Since it's difficult to make adjustments during an actual performance, the actor relies on a director or coach during rehearsals. Children need feedback even more than professionals. Thus, the teacher's job in any stage activity must be to play director to the students, or to train them to direct each other. This means giving honest reactions: laughing only if the joke is funny, asking for clearer enunciation if the performers are mumbling, demanding "bigger voices" if the show isn't reaching the outskirts of the audience.

No amount of rehearsal, however, can shield the performer from the audience's emotions once the act goes on. This electricity gives actors a heightened sense of self, even a feeling of power. It can be intoxicating. It can be overwhelming.

Conviction

One key element of stage presence goes by many names: concentration, getting into the role, believing, conviction. The importance of this concept is illustrated by Stanislavsky's reaction to an improvisation he once did with a student. The situation was: two enemy spies meeting in a restaurant—one, played by the student, was trying to poison the other, played by Stanislavsky. After a few moments of small talk, the younger spy pointed offstage and

said, "Say, look at that horse out the window." When the older spy turned, the youth slipped poison into his drink. A moment later, he proposed a toast. The older spy, reaching for his glass, knocked it over.

The student suddenly jumped up and pointed to the spilled drink. "You've ruined everything!" he shouted. But Stanislavsky only laughed and explained that it was the pupil who had spoiled things. A real spy would not have incriminated himself so readily.

Drama theorists remind us that no stage performance can work unless the audience makes an effort to "suspend disbelief." But the real effort is that of the performer, the person who must *acquire* belief in what he or she is doing. It is the performer, not the audience, who really knows what's going on, who has to struggle, focus attention, and exercise belief in the face of pretense, to make the act come across as actual.

Activities

Two theatrical agents met at a carnival to see an act everyone was raving about. As the audience watched in awed silence, Bosco the Great climbed up a ladder to a tiny pedestal, four hundred feet in the air. He took a deep breath, then started to flap his arms up and down. The drums rolled, the cymbals crashed, and Bosco leaped off the pedestal and actually flew! His arms pumping madly, he circled the entire arena. Then, as he completed a loop-the-loop, one of the agents turned to the other and asked, "Is that all he does, bird imitations?"

—An Old Joke

For some people, like our jaded theatrical agent, only the super-colossal qualifies as a true stage event. We believe otherwise. On a modest scale (off off off off-Broadway), kids can become kings, astronauts, animals, historical figures, bus drivers, and inventors. They can stage complicated processes like blood circulation or hard-to-visualize concepts like loneliness or democracy.

Teachers who fail to use such activities in their daily curricula are probably still defining stage as the traditional "class play," with its fully costumed actors reciting fully memorized dialogue. Perhaps surprisingly, we have not even included this kind of production in the present chapter. Instead, we've concentrated on forms that can be produced right in the classroom, that can tie into the curriculum without becoming a curriculum in themselves, and that can be done masterfully by children.

The Oral Narrative

Over the last several decades, the major thrust of literacy instruction in schools has been to teach reading as a private, silent process whose major function is efficient information-gathering. This kind of reading is to literature what the superhighway is to touring. It gets you there fast, but you don't see much along the way.

The roots of literature, however, are not silent but oral. The great narrative poems (*Beowulf, Gilgamesh, The Iliad*) existed for centuries in purely spoken form before they were written down. One presumes that the writing came easily because wrong-sounding, unmoving, unmemorable phrases had long since been discarded. There is no such thing as a piece of writing which "looks" great on paper but "sounds" false when read aloud. Experienced authors have an aural sense of the words they write even when composing silently, just as the mature, deaf Beethoven knew the sound of the music he composed.

Students who have been conditioned to ignore the sound of literature, who treat print as if it were a tongueless medium, can hardly be expected to write meaningful sentences, let alone prose that flows and lives. There is a place for silent reading, just as there is a place for the superhighway. But children should also have the opportunity to voice stories and poems and thus appreciate the sensual, rhythmic qualities of literature.

"Story hour" is the simplest sort of oral narrative for children to perform. The material can be handled in three ways: read from a book, spoken verbatim from memory, or recited in the storyteller's own words. In each case, the speaker is a one-person troupe, interpreting the material, gesturing, differentiating the voices. Baby Bear, you know, sounds nothing at all like Papa Bear. And anyone who is going to tell us about the "tell-tale" heart had better not be calm about it.

Obviously, we're talking about something very different from having kids, one-after-the-other, sight read aloud from a text while the rest follow (or don't follow) along in the book. Successful oral reading requires familiarity with the material—in a word, rehearsal.

One logical extension of "story hour" is termed "readers' theater." Here, the various parts in a printed play are taken by different actors. The cast sits facing the audience and does a "reading" from scripts they hold in their hands. Usually everyone

appears in street clothes. Gesture and facial expression are minimized.

Many traditional plays adapt easily to readers' theater. So does published dialogue from famous trials, Senate hearings, and weekly news shows. Transcripts from *Meet the Press*,° for example, could be performed as a monthly current events activity. Another rich and readily available source of material is the transcribed interview of the sort found in popular magazines. These give kids a chance to voice-play famous sports stars, writers, artists, business leaders, entertainers, and politicians.

A third oral form is "poetry performance," sometimes done to jazz or other background music. Most people who love and understand the spoken word have favorite language bits, usually poems, on the tips of their tongues. Often this results from natural, self-imposed familiarity with the material, though there's certainly nothing wrong with kids consciously memorizing, if it's done in the right spirit. Students who have internalized great passages from *The Bible*, Shakespeare, modern poetry, or popular songs lead a rich verbal life, even in silences.°

The Mime Show

Mime is the art of telling a story through gesture, movement, and facial expression. More than any other, this act tests the limits of nonverbal communication. At once, it teaches us to appreciate words and to appreciate how much the body alone can convey.

Pure mime is harder than it looks. While almost anyone can successfully imitate the act of peeling and eating a banana, the novice's attempt to silently portray a firefighter getting dressed and sliding down the pole is likely to be interpreted as an octopus shaking hands with a clam.

The solution is easy: don't dwell on "pure" mime, especially for openers. Instead, start with charades, where there are conventional gestures for "it sounds like," "it's a little word," etc. Another approach is "story theater," in which someone tells a story while mimes act it out on the stage. This is a good beginning stage activity because the performers do not have to memorize lines or control their voices.

Once they get the hang of it, students will want to try more ambitious acts. Almost any situation can be mimed. San Francisco's famous "Toad the Mime" has performed the following bits: a nightmare, the theft of a watermelon from a supermarket, a person trying to escape from a box, a satire of a familiar TV commercial, two lonely people trying to make friends, and the creation of the world.

Besides using music to suggest a mood, Toad gives each bit a name and sometimes describes the situation briefly in words before miming it. Some critics might condemn this as "impure" mime, but it permits the audience to spend less time trying to guess what's going on and more time enjoying the execution.

The Puppet Show

Few stage activities have more potential scope than puppet shows. With almost no outlay of cash, the puppeteer can create entire worlds: oceans, deserts, jungles, palaces, dungeons, outer space. All that's required are a few mini-backdrops.

Casting is no problem. The smallest kid can play the giant. A ten-year-old Romeo with more braces than teeth can smooch without fear. And even shy children can step forth to play bold heroes since they'll be exposing just the voice part of their bodies.

The only drawback is that some students may assume that the format can handle only fairy tales and other kids' stuff. Tell them that some fifty years ago a San Francisco puppeteer, Ralph Chesse, was producing Elizabethan dramas and romantic operas for adult audiences. One critic called his *Hamlet* "a production of rare beauty." Another said it caught the mood of Shakespearean tragedy "more completely than any of the numerous stage productions I have witnessed."

During a production of the opera *Hansel and Gretel*, Chesse discovered just how gripping his puppet programs could be. A charge of flash powder in the witch's oven set the curtains on fire, and the puppeteers had to interrupt their work to rip down the curtains and beat out the flames on the tiny stage. As Chesse recalled, "Strangely enough, it proved to be a rather effective ending. People in the audience came up to us after the play and said it was awe-inspiring seeing those huge hands reaching down, as if some sort of divine intervention were taking place. . . . During those few hours while the play was in progress, the audience lived within the dimensions of the puppet stage. More than that: even when the real world intervened, it was the *illusion* that prevailed. The hands were out of proportion, not the figures onstage."

With almost no outlay of cash, the puppeteer can create entire worlds.

The Puppets. Puppets should not be life-like in appearance. Imitating the human form invites a direct comparison with nature. Nature always wins. Audiences may find "realistic" puppets cute, attractive, even amazing, but they will not find them convincing.

Instead, a puppet should be more like a three-dimensional cartoon, with the visual emphasis on a few particular features—say, the eyes and the hair. With costume, too, a single focusing element (top hat, large earrings, red cape) is preferable to a complete scaled-down outfit.

Hand puppets are the best type for classroom productions. They are available in stores, but if you create your own you can tailor the puppet to the story rather than vice versa. Make the body (torso and arms) by sewing two pieces of cloth together. Fashion heads from wood, clay, papier-mâché, plaster, or styrofoam balls. It's best if the head is hollow so it can be manipulated by the puppeteer's fingers. Unusual characters call for unusual heads—a light bulb (genius), a tin can (robot), a tennis ball (sports fan), a piece of fruit (nutrition expert), a Halloween skull-candle (ghoul). For eyes, ears, and so forth, use household items like thumb tacks, washers, bottle caps, and buttons.

The Stage. With some assistance from a carpentry-minded parent, you should have no trouble erecting a wooden puppet stage in your classroom, complete with curtains and lights. If you don't want to bother assembling something from scratch, simply cut a hole in a large cardboard box or packing crate.

The Sets. Like the puppets themselves, sets should be suggestive rather than realistic. Simple, easy to identify props—a rainbow, a mountain, a tree—usually work better than detailed backgrounds. For materials, consider stick-on stars, yarn, silver foil, oaktag, and other household whatnots.

The Acting. The challenge of puppetry is giving life to the inanimate. If the puppeteer relaxes for a moment, the puppet dies. To keep the puppet animated, the puppeteer must always feel himself onstage. This is relatively easy when the puppet is talking or performing a bit of business. But even when the puppet is standing motionless, maybe listening to another character, the puppeteer's fingers must stay tense to keep the creature from going flaccid.

The Directing. Perhaps more than onstage performers, puppeteers need a director's feedback since they cannot see what they are doing. The director's job is to inform the actors whether it is clear which puppet is talking, whether the voices are sufficiently individualized, whether the gestures can be read, and whether the characters interact convincingly.

A puppet should be more like a three-dimensional cartoon.

Uncle Sam gives an autobiographical talk. This puppet by Deidre Bryant, age 13, was sewn together from felt scraps. The stage is an old radio with its innards removed. Junked television sets also convert readily to puppet theaters.

The Material. Students can produce ready-made puppet plays or they can try adapting "live actor plays" to the miniature stage. More important in the school context, they can whip up their own original dramas based on history, biography, comics, fiction, or current events. As three hundred years of Punch and Judy have proved, the format is outstanding for slapstick humor. But it also seems ripe for fantasy, science fiction, and other exotic concepts. And, of course, there is the ever-popular puppet-and-live-actor routine, à la Kukla, Fran and Ollie, and ventriloquism acts.

The Speech

The opportunity to give a speech usually results in more stuttering than oratory. While for some people getting up before a group is as easy and pleasurable as talking with a good friend, most of us feel embarrassed just giving our names at a PTA meeting.

Part of the trouble is that the phrase "unaccustomed as I am to public speaking" is usually true. Since speech-making costs nothing, one might expect it to be practiced weekly if not daily by students of all ages. Instead, like the rack, it is saved for special occasions.

The problem is that schools too often regard the speech as an end in itself. The student approaches the podium not because he or she has something to say, but because it is oral book-report time. There is no reason for the speech except to give a speech.

In the real world, speeches start from the speech-maker's need to communicate. Specifically, this can be to: 1) share information, 2) mold opinion, 3) stir people to action, 4) entertain, 5) make money—or any mix of the above. To get kids making authentic speeches, try to establish an environment in which they have reasons to express themselves publicly.

Certainly in the classroom there is plenty to talk about. Sometimes the text can be borrowed. In a science class studying evolution, for example, a student might deliver one of the famous courtroom speeches from *Inherit the Wind.* More often, kids will want to invent their own speeches: a guest lecture that Giordano Bruno might have given on his controversial cosmology, or maybe a pep talk in which a vaccine rallies its forces against an invading virus.

Planning the Speech. Whether you write out your speech or ad-lib it, four tips for handling the content are:

Grab interest fast. It's much easier to win an audience's attention at the beginning than at the end. Questions make good openers ("Would you believe . . . ?"). So do concrete images ("A man once fell from an airplane . . ."). So do jokes.

Be brief. A good working assumption is that there never was a speech that was too short. The most famous speech ever delivered in America, "The Gettysburg Address," uses only 267 words to sweep over eighty-seven years of history, analyze a war, and peer into the future.

Plan the ending. Some speakers stop when they discover they have nothing else to say: "Well, I guess that's it . . ." Hardly the way to elicit cheers.

Be clear. Listeners often can't or won't interrupt a speaker to ask that a point be clarified. Like writers, speech-makers should value directness and simplicity. An old rule advises: tell them what you're going to tell them, tell them, then tell them what you told them. The trick is to do this without being boring, repetitious, or condescending.

Rehearsing the Speech. Like a play, a speech needs rehearsing, whether it's to be read, delivered from memory, or improvised on the basis of prepared notes. The speaker must know the material and decide ahead of time how to handle it—reverently, jokingly, lightly, soberly. Rehearsals should cover gesture, posture, and audio-visual aids. One technique is to have the student first give the speech to a single friend, then to a small group, and finally to the target audience. This helps eliminate stage fright.

Checking the Auditorium. It's difficult enough to hold onto an audience without competition from a freezing room, bad acoustics, outside noise, or poor lighting. Experienced speakers ready the room, clearing unnecessary furniture off the stage, testing the microphone, and opening or closing windows. Lines like "I don't see the screen they promised, so I guess I'll have to show the slides on this tapestry" do not win curtain calls.

As always, improvement requires experience. Once your kids gain confidence, set up a speakers' bureau. Let other teachers know you have students who can talk on topics ranging from fixing bikes to Victorian poetry. Don't limit the circuit to your school. We know of a junior high group who, after several months of studying the relationship between lung cancer and smoking, went on a speaking tour of all the elementary schools in their district.

The Improvisation

The improvisation involves three challenges: 1) getting inside a character, 2) thinking on one's feet (the word "improvise" comes from the Latin "not foreseen"), and 3) creating plot and dialogue.

Viewed as a tool for exploring character and plot, improvisation requires only rudimentary props and costumes. A table, some chairs, and a pitcher give you a restaurant. A white towel equals the waiter's outfit.

The starting point is what professionals call "the minimal situation," a brief declaration of the characters, the setting, and the problem. In the Stanislavsky bit mentioned earlier, the minimal situation was: two spies in a restaurant, one trying to poison the other. Minimal situations can be drawn from almost any source—history, current events, a comic strip, a song, a happening observed on the way to school, a piece of fiction, or an interpersonal problem in the classroom.

Certain troupes, like San Francisco's *Committee* and Boston's *The Proposition*, have developed the amazing ability to take a minimal situation from the audience and use it as the basis of a complete improvised playlet. A less demanding approach is to work out the improvisation before performing it. Start with a short story or novel. A small group reads the work, then breaks it into scenes. The parts are cast, and the players begin improvising the dialogue and action until everyone has a good idea of how each moment will play. Eventually, costumes and sets are added, making the drama ready for an audience. The effect is one of controlled spontaneity, each performance free-floating and slightly different from the last, a style that can be as enchanting as a jazz improvisation on a familiar melody.

A more complex and sustained variation on the improvisation is "the simulation." One simulation we've had success with, "The Alien Visitors," asks students to play beings from another planet. Their task is to plan and carry out an investigation of life on earth. The aliens can tape interviews with earthlings, take photographs, gather artifacts, and study TV shows, radio broadcasts, magazines, and newspapers. The specific methodologies and powers of the aliens are decided by the students before starting the simulation. In the end—after about a week—the aliens must decide whether Earth represents a danger to interplanetary peace. If the answer is yes, Earth will be destroyed in as "humane" a manner as possible. Whatever the decision, students can publish their findings as research booklets or hold public slide shows for "aliens" throughout the school.

Simulation can be used to explore almost any curriculum area. Examples: a *press conference* in which reporters question Lincoln the day before his speech at Gettysburg; an *interview* between Freud and a patient; an *interrogation* of a World War I spy; a *trial* such as those of Socrates, Jesus, Calley, and Dreyfus (the latter in French for advanced French students); a *discussion* between Christopher Columbus and Neil Armstrong; and *debates* between Thomas Jefferson and Alexander Hamilton, between Ptolemy and Copernicus, between Karl Marx and Andrew Carnegie, or among Supreme Court Justices during *Marbury vs. Madison*. The only rules are to be factually accurate (research the topic) and to bring the simulation to a definite conclusion (plan an ending). Several curriculum-development groups regularly publish highly structured simulations, usually called "simulation games," that can last several days and deal with matters like war, economics, politics, and the environment.°

The Magic Act

The same cynics who get their kicks convincing little kids that there is no Santa Claus and that a rainbow is just water refracting sunlight also spread the dismal mistruth that there is no magic. When they see the magician turn a handkerchief into a dove, they deny their senses and declare, "He didn't really do it. It's just a trick." For them, the magician is a fake. How they miss the point!

The magician, in fact, is like a poet or a teacher. Using manual dexterity, props, verbal patter, and an understanding of human nature, he or she kindles our sense of wonder and awakens us with mystery. Seen this way, nothing could be more real than magic.

Magic can encompass many classroom topics. There is *number* magic. . .

> *For this trick, you need a blackboard and a piece of chalk. Have an audience volunteer come up on the stage. Instruct him to write any number he wants on the blackboard, but before he does, blindfold yourself or face away from him so you cannot see his choice. Tell your subject to do the following things to the number:*
>
> *1. Double it.*
> *2. Add "8."*
> *3. Divide the result in half.*
> *4. Subtract the original number.*
>
> *Before you look at the blackboard for the first time, predict that the answer is "four." (It will be, no matter what number was selected.)*

The one thing that isn't magical about magic is learning how to do it.

There is *psychology* magic. . .

This is a mind-reading act. You will need an assistant who first blindfolds you to prove you aren't receiving visual cues. The assistant goes into the audience, and a volunteer whispers a number into his ear—any between 1 and 9,999. After returning to the stage, the assistant sits on a chair and you place a hand on one or both of his temples. Eventually, you are able to "read his thoughts" and announce the correct number. The trick is that the assistant "counts off" each digit of the number by moving the back of his jaw in a biting motion, thus bulging the muscle in each temple. One bite = 0. Two bites = 1. Three = 2. And so on. (If the number is 904, the assistant would count off ten, pause, count off one, pause, then count off five.)

There is *science* magic. . .

You need a coin, a match, a thin drinking glass, a comb, and some hair on your head. Very carefully, balance the coin on its side and lay the match— ever so gently—on the edge of the coin. Carefully set the glass over this arrangement. What you have to do now is make the match fall off the coin without:

1. Moving, lifting, or touching the glass . . .
2. Disturbing any cloth or covering that happens to be on the table . . .
3. Touching the table . . .
4. Stamping the floor . . .
5. Moving the coin in any way.

And yet it is possible. Take a comb and run it briskly through your hair several times. Then hold the comb close against the glass without moving the glass. The match will fall mysteriously as the comb touches the glass.

Performing stage magic at almost any level of sophistication will teach children important lessons in human behavior and perception (or, rather, misperception). They'll discover that believing is not necessarily seeing.

The one thing that isn't magical about magic is learning how to do it. Like a sonata that seems to flow effortlessly from a pianist's fingers, a "simple" card disappearance may require days of practice. The best way to learn is the apprenticeship method. Try locating helpful magicians through magic shops listed in the Yellow Pages or through the Assembly of the Society of American Magicians, founded in 1902 and once headed by Houdini.°

The Comedy Routine

Through a glass lightly, comedians help us to see the world. Humor, like logic, is not so much a truth in itself as a way of making things clear.

Unlike logic, humor is generally regarded as an inappropriate mode for exploring the academic disciplines. Yet, in the real world, comedians often reveal great and little truths about subject matter in the course of their routines. Tom Lehrer, for example, has turned the New Math and the Periodic Table of the Elements into patter songs. Much of Bob Newhart's best remembered material is based on the lives of historical figures like George Washington and the Wright Brothers. Talk show hosts rely on current events for many of their jokes.

Comedy in the classroom begins with the student seeing the humorous possibilities in some curriculum issue. In a foreign language class it might be "baseball through the eyes of an ancient Roman." In a math class it might be "the imaginary numbers." In a driver education class it might be "an undertaker voices his opposition to automobile safety."

Next, the student should prepare his routine. In most cases, this means the three R's of researching, writing, and rehearsing. Some kids may find they have a knack for ad libbing around the topic, particularly in collaboration with one or two peers. This approach still requires rehearsals, during which the students agree on an ending and practice helping each other stick to the subject. When presenting their polished routines before the class, students should keep the following pointers in mind:

Tell only those jokes you find funny, not those you think others will find funny. It's almost impossible to get a laugh with a story that has never delighted you personally.

Never memorize a routine in someone else's words. The comic's job is to be funny, not just to say funny things.

Use dialects only if you have a flair for them. If you can't pull off a British accent, don't mumble at it, then apologize and ask the audience to imagine the right effect. Better to do the routine straight.

Polish the timing. Comedy is based on rhythm, the sense of pacing a story and hitting the punch line at precisely the right moment.

Don't laugh at your own jokes. Like performing seals, some comedians applaud themselves. This can sometimes be infectious, but more often it's just distracting. A simple smile or deadpan expression is usually best.

Standards

One of the authors visited a fourth grade classroom in a school known for its bright kids and innovative approaches. Half a dozen students were putting on a classroom simulation of a Roman Senate meeting.

The effect was literally unbelievable. These normally beautiful, intelligent, and graceful children were standing awkwardly about, giggling, staring at their friends in the audience and, in general, seeming embarrassed about the whole thing. It looked like Rome the day after the fall.

Now, no one expects kids to behave like seasoned Broadway actors, but any stage performer can strive for certain basic standards. The above-described "spectacle" suggests a few things to avoid:

Self-Consciousness. Most of us have had the weird experience of suddenly, in the middle of a conversation, hearing our own voices and feeling alienated from ourselves. We may lose track of what we've been saying or fumble what we're doing. Stage heightens this self-consciousness. The performer, often wearing an eye-catching costume, stands physically apart, trapped in a beam of light, the target of stares. His every word is listened to, whereas in normal life people are usually more interested in hearing themselves than others.

It is difficult to be natural in such unnatural circumstances, and telling kids to relax just makes them nervous. The solution is to let them have gradual but continual audience exposure. This means making stage a regular rather than a special activity. It also suggests starting with less revealing formats like puppetry and mime and keeping audiences small, even smaller than class size.

Awkward Entrances. There is a world of difference between offstage and onstage, though the distance between them may be no wider than the thickness of the curtain. Moving into view of the audience can hit the performer like a leap into an icy

Telling kids to relax just makes them nervous.

lake. The answer is for actors to think themselves "on stage" before physically arriving there. This means not only "getting into character" but anticipating the feel of the audience and leaning forward to greet it a few seconds before appearing.

Misused Eye Contact. In dramatic acting, it is almost always a mistake for a performer to make eye-contact with the audience. Eye-contact is so powerful a means of communication that it pulls the act off the stage and into our laps. In other kinds of stage performances—lectures, comedy routines, magic shows—it is a mistake to *avoid* eye contact with the audience. Here, eye-contact helps get the message across.

Forgotten Lines. The interesting thing about the phenomenon of forgetting lines (or "going up" as they say in the theater) is that unless the audience knows the play by heart, they will have no idea who is at fault. The other actors must come to your rescue or everyone ends up looking bad. One of the hardest stage disciplines for a child to master is not going to pieces when he forgets a line, but to behave instead as if he is still in control and to wait for another actor or a prompter to feed him a clue. ("I know what you're thinking, Merton, you're thinking that. . . .") The kind of teamwork involved when performers help one another through an act is one of the most important payoffs of stage in the classroom, a needed alternative to individualized competition.

Unmodulated Delivery. Rate and volume of speech are crucial in making a performance convincing. Speaking too slowly or too softly is sometimes a result of nervousness, but more often these errors stem from a simple lack of awareness that the speed and "size" of a delivery can be consciously controlled.

In rehearsal, the student might practice delivering the same line or speech at various extremes. First he should do it as loudly (or "big," as a professional director might say) as possible. Then as softly. Then as fast. Then as slowly. Then he should experiment with various combinations (loudly and slowly, etc.). Chances are, the performer will have no trouble determining which kind of delivery best serves the material.

When kids begin to break away from the mumbling and diffidence that characterize non-acting, they often go to the other extreme. Exaggerated, hammy shouting and gesticulating in theater is sometimes called *declamation.* While not to be con-

The teamwork involved when performers help one another through an act is one of the most important payoffs of stage in the classroom.

fused with real acting, declamation is preferable to diffidence, for the simple reason that it is easier to tone down a performance than build it up. *Projection*, the art of acting naturally and unselfconsciously and yet making your voice and gestures travel across a theater, does not come easily to most children and must be learned over time.

Not Picking Up Cues. Many amateurs take the last word of the speech before theirs as the cue to begin speaking. The result is to make the audience feel as if they could play a quick game of canasta between any two speeches in the show. Theater directors generally refer to purposeless pauses between lines as "not picking up your cues."

As in actual conversation, an actor should "decide" what he will say next not at the *end* of someone's last sentence, but in the *middle* of it. He is then ready to leap in as soon as the person is finished—maybe before. In rehearsal, kids should play around with interrupting each other and saying their lines at the same time. Some of their experimentation might even end up in the finished act.

One of the most common causes of pointless pauses in acting is the "divided" or "unfinished" line. Here's an example:

Fred: The last time I was in a jam like this was back in 1932, in the Amazon, when old Bastido and I were trying to . . . (pause)

Lewis: Fred, I've got it!

Amateurs typically read a line like Fred's exactly the way it appears on paper, rather than the way Fred would say it in real life. The actor's tone of voice reveals he is *expecting* to be interrupted. The solution is for the first actor to have in mind several words beyond those provided by the author. This further forestalls disaster in the event that Lewis forgets his cue and is late in producing the interruption.

The other sworn enemies of real-life acting are exclamatory phrases like "Lo!" and "Hold!" and "Ha, ha, ha!" Children have an exceptionally difficult time knocking the stilts out from under such expressions and getting them to sound like respectable members of a natural, spontaneous conversation. Remember that the dialogue in any stage performance, including "readings" of plays, should *not* sound like it's being read. The goal is always to get those lines off the printed page and comfortably onto the tongue.

The question is: Can regular kids, not just theater prodigies, bring stage off? Can they be stage-real? The answer is: Go watch a couple of pre-schoolers playing house with dolls. Or a bunch of eight-year-

Can regular kids, not just theater prodigies, bring stage off? Can they be stage-real?

olds being cops and robbers—watch them slink and dart and die. They can scream and laugh quicker than a Broadway actress, for children have direct access to their emotions.

The trouble is that stage, so natural to kids outside the school, hasn't been allowed inside. Invite it in, be gentle with the audience problem, and let the kids act, act, act. It will be child's play for them.

Sources and Resources

1. Transcripts from *Meet the Press* are available for 15 cents each from Merkel Press, P.O. Box 2111, Washington, D.C. 20013.

2. An anthology of poems particularly suited to performance is *Sounds & Silences: Poems for Performing* by Robert W. Boynton and Maynard Mack (Rochelle Park, NJ: Hayden Book Co., 1975).

3. The standard collection of practical drama activities is Viola Spolin's *Improvisation for the Theater* (Evanston, IL: Northwestern University Press, 1963).

4. An excellent collection of simulations and games is *Human Communication Handbook: Simulations and Games* by Brent D. Ruben and Richard W. Budd (Rochelle Park, NJ: Hayden Book Co., 1974). One of the best booklets on simulation games is *Teaching about Spaceship Earth: A Role-playing Experience for the Middle Grades*, available from Intercom, 218 East 18th Street, New York, NY 10003. A unique, on-going source of information about the field is *Simulation/Gaming News*. Send subscription inquiries to Box 3039, University Station, Moscow, ID 83843.

5. Louis Phillips, a magician friend of ours, suggests the following magic books for beginners:

General

a. *This Is My First Magic Book, So I'm a Little Nervous* by Bob Einstein (New York: Grosset and Dunlap, 1971).

b. *John Fischer's Magic Book* by John Fischer (Englewood Cliffs, NJ: Prentice-Hall, 1971).

c. *Wide World of Magic* by Vincent H. Gaddes (New York: Criterion Books).

d. *100 of Scarne's Magic Tricks* by John Scarne (New York: Cornerstone Library).

Mathematical

e. *Mathematics, Magic and Mystery* by Martin Gardner (New York: Dover Publications).

f. *Math & Magic* by Royal Vale Heath (New York: Dover Publications, 1953).

Historical

g. *Panorama of Magic* by Milbourne Christopher (New York: Dover Publications, 1962).

h. *Houdini: The Untold Story* by Milbourne Christopher (New York: Pocket Books, 1970).

Design: 4
Drawing as a second language

Anyone who has ever had his imagination stirred by a science fiction comic book or his beliefs challenged by a political cartoon knows that design can have all the power and richness of the newer communications forms. It is every bit as electrifying as television or film.

While our definition of design does not rule out oil painting, woodcuts, lithography, and other traditional graphic arts, the focus here will be on projects that can be done outside your school's art room. Whether the student is visualizing a Civil War battle, abstracting the structure of a city, or diagramming how a computer works, you don't need to be an art teacher to help him learn through design.

In *The Great Comic Book Heroes*,° Jules Feiffer describes the thrill that inevitably accompanies a dedicated child's first experiences with one particularly dynamic design activity: making comic books. While the youthful Feiffer's peers were passively devouring comic books without worrying how they were put together, he was "counting how many frames there were to a page, how many pages there were to a story—learning how to form, for my own use, phrases like: @X#?/ . . ."

Eventually Feiffer found employment in the schlock houses that during the 1940s ground out low-grade comic books. Typically, he and his fellow cartoonists would have to work on weekends in one of their apartments. "If the place being used had a kitchen, black coffee was made and remade. If not, coffee and sandwiches were sent for—no matter the hour. In midtown Manhattan something always had to be open. Except on Sundays. A man could look for hours before he found an open delicatessen. The other artists sat working, starving: some dozing over their breadboards, others stretching out for a nap on the floor, their empty fingers twitching to the rhythm of the brush . . . This was the birth of a new art form! A lot of talk about that: how to design better, draw better, animate a figure better, so that it would jump, magically, off the page. Movies on paper —the final dream!"

This kind of passionate belief in one's work can become part of the classroom experience. Authentic learning inevitably follows. Imagine your kids designing a futuristic metropolis—solving problems of transportation, overcrowding, and pollution-control as any city planner must do. Imagine that tawdry, fantastically popular little narrative form called the comic book having its face scrubbed (but only a little bit) and being used by your students to tell original stories or dramatize history. Imagine a student "science report" in which the pictures are not the usual frosting on the text but actually *are* the text. (When Watson and Crick decided to announce their concept of the DNA molecule, they published a very short article in which all the essential content was contained in diagrams.) It's simply a matter of legitimizing design forms in schools, the way they are legitimized in real-world science and art, so that the student can use them in his education without feeling he is being softheaded or avoiding a truly meaty medium like print.

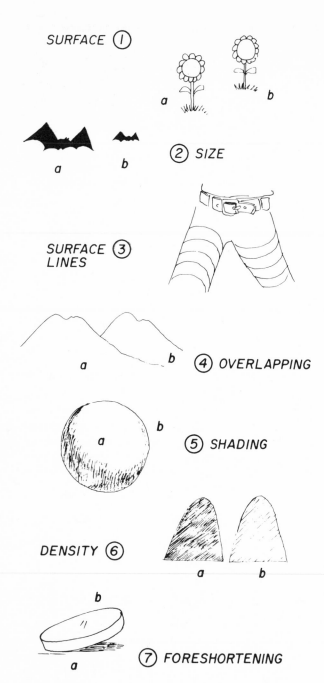

SURFACE ①

② SIZE

SURFACE ③
LINES

④ OVERLAPPING

⑤ SHADING

DENSITY ⑥

⑦ FORESHORTENING

Creating the illusion of depth: Bruce McIntyre's seven laws of perspective are seen in isolation (top) and working together (bottom).

Concepts

This chapter is subtitled "Drawing as a Second Language" because once students learn how to draw —that is, make representational pictures—they will have mastered most of the key principles of design, such as line, shape, overlapping, depth, balance, and unity. (Color is an important exception, but it lies beyond the scope of this book.) Learning "how to draw" is a peculiar notion in our culture. The common assumption is that unless a child is born with a talent for making iconographic images on paper, he will never learn how to draw, and there is no point trying to teach him.

We reject this assumption. While not all children have the potential to become artists, most can acquire enough skill to use drawing freely in their school studies and their personal lives. Print offers an analogous situation. Not all children have the potential to become novelists, but most learn how to write.

Of course, learning to draw, like learning to write, is an ambitious undertaking. It requires practice. If you are an elementary teacher, formal drawing lessons can be a valuable way to use the time blocked out in your curriculum for "art"—at least as valuable as the usual mucking around with fingerpaints and linoleum blocks, and much more effective in giving children this important second language.

One of the best attempts to organize the principles of drawing is "The Audio-Visual Drawing Program" created by Bruce McIntyre,° a Disney artist turned elementary school teacher. The rest of this section explains McIntyre's concepts of perspective, position, and alignment. We've also included some of his specific drawing lessons. The idea is to get you and your students drawing freely and often, whether from models, from memory, or from imagination.

Perspective

McIntyre believes that the essence of drawing is creating an illusion of depth. For him, perspective is a set of "laws which cause some things in a picture to appear closer to you or farther from you than others." These laws, derived from careful observation of objects in the real world, are: surface, size, surface lines, overlapping, shading, density, and foreshortening.

Surface. Think of the paper you are drawing on as a surface. Objects and parts of objects drawn near the bottom of this surface generally look closer than those drawn near the top.

Size. Objects or parts of objects drawn larger than other objects or parts of objects will also look closer.

Surface Lines. Wrapping curved lines around part of an object helps give it a sense of depth.

Overlapping. An overlapping object or part of an object looks closer than an object or part being overlapped.

Shading. Shading part of an object helps give it a sense of depth.

Density. An object or part of an object that is drawn darker and with more detail usually looks more dimensional and closer than an object or part that is not.

Foreshortening. When "flattened" or oblong shapes are used in representing objects whose surfaces have symmetrical or parallel contours, then the picture's feeling of depth will be increased. It is especially important to learn to draw the foreshortened circle (a "cigar shape" or "flat circle") and the foreshortened square (a "diamond shape" or "flat square").

Position

Novice artists generally select the vantage point which makes their subjects appear to have only two dimensions. Ironically, the "flat-on" or "head-on" perspective is the exception to everyday perceptual experience. The number of potential three-dimensional views of an object is, in fact, infinite.

According to McIntyre, you can overcome the habit of rendering your subject in flat profile by consciously positioning it on the paper so that it points in one of eight particular "directions."

Alignment

McIntyre teaches alignment to "show how to line things up in three-dimensional drawing." Alignment is necessary when drawing a series of parallel objects, such as telephone poles, cracks in a sidewalk, or legs on a table.

Sometimes you can accomplish alignment in your head. At other times, you will want to sketch in light "alignment lines" which are later erased. The basic lines, all of which extend in either Direction 1 (northeast) or Direction 7 (northwest), are shown in the alignment diagram on this page.

Activities

With nothing more technological than a pencil and a piece of paper, kids can immerse themselves in the pleasures of the design medium. They can draw new life forms (aliens, animals, plants), environments (planets, classrooms, amusement parks), and

The naive artist's "flat-on" perspective versus the kind of three-dimensional view that characterizes common perceptual experience.

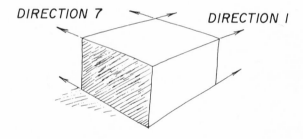

Eight conventional positions, selected for convenience out of an infinite number of valid possibilities.

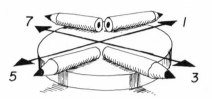

Proper alignment means that parallel elements must all point in the same direction.

Simple candle. *Start with a very small foreshortened circle ("cigar shape") at the top. In drawing the base, be sure to begin the big foreshortened circle up a little bit on the side of the candle.*

Jack-in-the-box. *This exercise begins with a foreshortened square ("diamond shape"). After sketching the box and the lid, place Jack in his box by drawing first his head, then his body (two lines going into the box from his head).*

Pencil in Direction 1 (northeast). *Five principles of drawing are used here:* surface *(the near end is closer to the bottom of the picture),* size *(the near end is drawn larger than the far end),* surface lines *(the black band around the pencil helps to make it look dimensional),* shading *(the underneath side of the pencil is shaded to help it turn under, away from the light), and* fore-shortening *(notice the foreshortened circle at the near end of the pencil).*

Flying saucer. *Start by drawing the glass dome. Now add a foreshortened circle around the base of the dome to form the platform. The body of the saucer is shallow. Notice that the back leg does not come down as far as the two near ones. Add the radar dish.*

Four-legged table. *Begin with a thick foreshortened square. Now draw straight lines down from the three corners, making the near one longer than the other two. At the bottom of the table, connect the ends of the legs with very light "alignment" lines. Finish the near leg by running a line down each side of the original line until you touch an alignment line. Then, starting at the end of each of the other two legs, follow the alignment lines inward toward the near leg for just a short distance. When you have drawn the thickness of the legs, draw up to the top of the table again. Now start in Direction 1 (northeast) from the end of the left leg and turn up. From the end of the right leg, start in Direction 7 (northwest) and turn up.*

6 Eight cans of spinach. *The purpose here is to learn over-lapping—drawing one thing behind another. Begin with the near can. Then, just above its two vertical edges, draw two more foreshortened circles and make cans out of them. Add more cans in the same way. Use shading on the left side of each can. By drawing the rear cans lighter, you are using another principle of drawing—density.*

7 Ball. *This is a shading exercise. Make the ball round by blending the shading as much as possible. Shading is normally placed underneath and on the left side of objects. Notice the foreshortened shadow below and slightly to the left of the ball.*

8 Small building with lean-to on each side. *Start with the foreshortened square. Draw a short line down from the two ends and extend the near corner all the way to the ground. At the bottom corner, start a line in Direction 1 and another in Direction 7. Draw a line on each side of the building just below roof, but not all the way across. Slant the lean-to roofs down. Complete their bottoms as though the roofs did not slant. All lines along the ground will be drawn in Direction 1 or Direction 7. Add the windows and shade.*

9 Observatory on hilltop with winding path. *Draw the building first, resting on a foreshortened piece of land. Then add one side of the path coming toward you. Be sure that the path is foreshortened and that the inside curves are sharper than the outside curves. Now add the opposite side of the path, making it wider as it comes toward you. Extend the sides of the hill from the apexes of the path.*

10 Grasshopper in Direction 3 (southeast). *Start with an oval-shaped head with an oval-shaped eye on the side. Line the right eye up with the left in Direction 1. Draw the nose-guard between the eyes. Behind her head is a saddle shape. Her front legs come out from between the saddle and head, bending like yours except that the feet are a series of segments. The middle legs bend opposite, coming out from the back of the saddle. Her jumping legs are behind the saddle. Line all the legs and feet up in Direction 1 and Direction 7. Her wings are drawn along her back in Direction 7. There are nine segments on her body, and the ovipositor on the tail end makes her a female.*

DESIGN · 49

artifacts (money, stamps, flags, toys, brochures, cereal boxes, bubble gum cards). In the real world, designers face such problems all the time. Take money. Not only does a need for currency arise whenever a new country is formed, but also whenever a Monopoly-like game is invented.

In the classroom, designing of this sort may be done for its own sake or as a preliminary step in executing models, miniatures, or prototypes. Such activities can reinforce subject-matter learning. Money-designing, for example, fits into social studies classes. Travel-brochure-designing fits into foreign language classes, animal-designing into biology classes, and amusement-park-ride-designing into physics classes. The remainder of this section explores eight major design formats.

The Illustration

Kids rarely bother to illustrate their print productions, whether fiction or nonfiction. And when they do, they know not to take the endeavor seriously since the grade will probably be based only on what they've written.

In the real world, on the other hand, the illustration of printed matter is a major concern. Almost every magazine, newspaper, or book publisher has an art staff. Pictures can draw attention to a story, clarify it, counterpoint it, or simply make the reading more enjoyable.

Students should approach the problem the way professionals do. The first step is reading the piece with an eye toward illustrating it. A short story set in a fantastical location, for example, might require a map. Next, the illustrator plans the layout—the quantity, sizes, and positions of the pictures. Finally, he chooses an apt medium (pencil, pen, crayon, fine-line marker) and executes the drawings.

Novice illustrators must overcome the temptation to draw right on the same paper that contains the text. Otherwise, if they botch the job, they'll have to redo the words as well as the drawings. A more efficient method is to perfect the pictures separately, then cut them out and paste them in their appropriate locations in the layout.

One important variation on the illustration is the "history painting" or "documentary drawing." Even in our age of the camera, there are times when only a designer's imagination can show us what an important event may have looked like. For example, during the height of the Watergate scandal, the editors of *New York* magazine became aware that, for all the media coverage accorded the event, readers were having trouble actually picturing the various arrests, payoffs, court hearings, and meetings. So several

Drawing a picture from scratch: note the erasure of guidelines after they are no longer needed.

artists were hired to "re-enact" Watergate in a series of documentary drawings.

In a history class, students can use this format to capture everything from the assassination of Lincoln to the building of Stonehenge. Class discussion can focus on probable accuracy and why the artist "interpreted" the event as he or she did. Documentary drawing also fits well into the study of science (an artist's conception of life on Neptune), mathematics (Pythagoras rotating his right triangles), and literature (the murder of the pawnbroker in *Crime and Punishment*).

The One-panel Cartoon

Publishers often classify cartoons as "filler," useful only for occupying leftover space. But as jelly is to a donut and stuffing to a turkey, cartoons can be a publication's most satisfying part.

While the one-panel cartoon has relevance throughout the curriculum, its natural spot is probably the current events class. Students can use it to epitomize their views of recent developments in culture, politics, science, and the arts. School affairs, too, are grist for the quill.

Whatever the topic, the starting point is usually a funny or poignant idea—a fact, a joke, an irony, a bit of wordplay—rather than a graphic image. The task is to convert this idea into a visual or a visual-verbal message. Students should sketch their cartoons in pencil, "ink" them in black and white or color using fineline markers, and erase the pencil lines. (Hesitant cartoonists might use ready-made pictures clipped out of magazines and newspapers.) The caption or gag line should be worked out separately and then added to the finished image.

The Comic Book

In the 1920s, booklets reproducing Sunday and daily comic strips from the newspapers began appearing on newsstands. By the early 1930s, so many reprint booklets were in circulation that there were no longer enough newspaper strips to go around. Editors were forced to use "all new" stories. Eventually, the "all new" stories took over, and the comic book was born.

The heritage of comic books, then, is narrative. Telling stories and presenting characters have always been what they do best. When you introduce the comic book or the comic strip as a form for solving problems in a science, history, or language class, the idea is not for students to produce panel by panel equivalents to educational television—you're not interested in pictures of instructors pointing at charts

Illustration for a piece of fictional history, "The Adventures of Nathan Blake in the New World," by Carol Heller, age 13 (top).

Political cartoon by Richard March, age 16, published in high school newspaper (bottom).

Comic strip by Laurel Brown, age 16. Even the reluctant artist can use the comic medium to capture events, ideas, and emotions.

of an artery, space capsule, or mead-hall. Instead, imagine a comic book *story* in which the main character *is* a blood cell or an astronaut or Beowulf.

Comics have a grammar all their own. While most of your kids have probably picked it up by now, it's a good idea to introduce the activity by reviewing concepts like panel and balloon. The "Professor Mindboggle" comic at the end of this chapter represents our attempt to explain these conventions to children. Feel free to reproduce it and pass it out.°

Comic book and comic strip production usually begins with the invention or borrowing of a main character: space creature, super-hero, buffoon, Aesop animal. After the baptism comes the thornier problem of making up an absorbing story line. Finally, the most ambitious phase—drawing.

If some of your students are reluctant artists, they can simplify the task by filling the panels with heads and dialogue balloons. Another solution is to create extremely abstract characters—characters who are nothing more than weird blobs or geometric shapes. Colors and patterns can help the reader to tell them apart.

Much current professional comic book and comic strip art is so complex it can be downright intimidating. But if you and your kids study historical examples, increasingly available via nostalgia reprints, you will discover that the first *Superman* and *Captain Marvel* comics were not drawn by great artists or even particularly good illustrators. Rather, they were drawn by people who cared about what they were doing and worked hard until they got better at it.°

Besides drawing, two aspects of comic book and comic strip production give children trouble: outlining the panels and using close-ups. The problem with panel-outlining is that some kids get so absorbed or frustrated by it they use up all their energy. Avoid this by passing out mimeographed sheets with six or eight same-size panels already ruled on them.

When children ignore or do not grasp the concept of "close-up" in comics, they end up showing us the same point of view on the action from one panel to the next. (Kids who do this also tend to squeeze all the content of a given panel into the bottom half only, which forces them to adopt a drawing style so cramped that the details become blurred and difficult to interpret.) Try showing the child how to "blow up" significant parts of the action—the face of a character as he says a key line, a hand holding a note—so that they occupy the entire panel. Since most close-ups are simpler to draw than "long shots," this technique can help the child to complete a full two or three page story in only a few hours.

The first "Superman" and "Captain Marvel" were not drawn by great artists, but by people who cared about what they were doing and worked hard to get better at it.

He saw Jane's bike,
walking down the street.

CAROL WILLIS

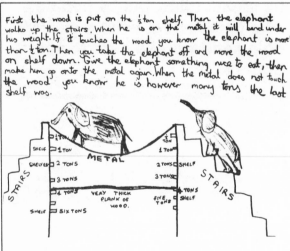

First the wood is put on the ½ ton shelf. Then the elephant walks up the stairs. When he is on the metal it will bend under his weight. If it touches the wood you know the elephant is more than ½ ton. Then you take the elephant off and move the wood on shelf down. Give the elephant something nice to eat, then make him go onto the metal again. When the metal does not touch the wood you know he is however many tons the last shelf was.

Instructional poster (top) by Carol Willis, age 16.

Diagram on how to weigh an elephant (bottom) by Anne Connelly, age 10.

The Poster

Because we usually observe them only in passing, posters must be grabby. Their makers seize our attention through simplicity—stark designs, bright colors, bold lettering, terse messages. Even "educational" posters, which have more leisurely exposure in classrooms and work areas, are most successful when designed to reach as well as teach.

The advent of watercolor markers has made it easy for students to create dynamic, colorful, broadline posters in the classroom or at home without prying esoteric materials from the art teacher. Rub-on letters, available in art supply stores, add a professional touch. Poster-making has many applications: travel posters in foreign language classes, theater posters in literature classes, wanted posters in social studies classes, advertising posters in English classes, how-to posters in physical education and home economics classes. Once the student has completed a poster, be sure to hang it somewhere in the school.

Classroom posters typically have two problems. First, the student has added unnecessary details. Second, his attempt to create solid, filled-in areas has ended in a congestion of unpleasing streaks and crosshatching.

One way around both problems is to produce the poster as a "photogram." Photograms can be prepared from any opaque material: construction-paper shapes, cut-out letters, and solid objects like leaves, flowers, keys, string, and spaghetti. The materials are laid out on the kind of inexpensive photographic paper whose tolerance for light is so great you can work with it right in the classroom. (Consult your local photo store.) The total arrangement is then sandwiched between glass sheets and exposed to sunlight or a bright photoflood bulb for five or ten minutes. The objects and cut-outs are removed and the paper is developed in a tray of water, fixed in a tray of fixer, and washed in another tray of water. The resulting poster will contain solid shapes wherever the opaque materials shielded it from the exposure-light.

The Diagram

Any drawing that explains a thing by symbolizing its parts and showing their relationships may be called a diagram. This includes maps, charts, graphs, floor plans, building plans, assembly plans, and blueprints. While most design products are interesting in and of themselves—we care more about da Vinci's painting of the Mona Lisa than we do about Mona —diagrams hold us only to the degree that they help us understand what they picture.

Kids learn a lot when they use diagrams to explain devices and processes: how an elevator moves, how a faucet works, how the local chess champion check-mated his opponent, how the home team scored the winning touchdown. More exciting still is using diagrams for original invention. Edward De Bono, a British philosopher, has shown that even very young children can concoct all sorts of machines on paper, from the folksy to the far-out. His books, *Children Solve Problems* and *The Dog Exercising Machine*, are filled with ingenious diagrams by kids in grades kindergarten on up.°

The Diorama

A diorama is a collection of related scale models grouped into a scene from human or natural history. Dioramas can be at once enchanting and practical. A miniature airport might be variously viewed by the general public as an entertaining waiting room display, by a child as a super-toy, and by an air traffic manager as a way to sell the community on runway expansion.

We have seen exciting student-made dioramas on such topics as city planning (a cardboard mock-up of Boston's Government Center), prehistoric animals, the Apollo 11 moon landing, the ancient Egyptian mummification process, the Battle of Concord Bridge, and the life cycle of the frog. For inspiration, kids should study the dioramas found in museums, science institutes, and architects' offices.

Students can construct the diorama's individual components—people, animals, vehicles, buildings—out of clay, wood, leather, and similar standbys. Store-bought toys and plastic model kits are also legitimate: the point is to design an authentic *setting* and *arrangement* for the figures. Landscapes and backdrops can be formed from natural materials like stones, twigs, and leaves, as well as from papier-mâché and cardboard. Kids might experiment with lighting their dioramas dramatically and adding prerecorded music, narration, or sound effects.

Although dioramas usually consist of scaled-down models, some have life-size elements. Natural history museums, for example, commonly feature taxidermy specimens. Thus, one version of this activity occurs when the student designs a dioramic display of her collection of insects, minerals, leaves, arrowheads, plants, or crayfish. But the subjects need not be dead, as demonstrated by aquariums, terrariums, flea circuses, and other mini-zoos.

The Exploratorium

From the funhouse to the planetarium, exploratoriums put their participants "on stage." In a school, an exploratorium is usually a series of interconnect-

Diorama of Battle at Concord Bridge (top) produced by second graders in Concord, Massachusetts.

Exploratorium (bottom) created by sixth graders of the Mariemont Elementary School, Sacramento, California.

ed spaces for people to walk or crawl through. Each time the participant rounds a corner, he confronts a new exhibit, demonstration, monster, or whatever. Exploratoriums can be built in closets, classrooms, or hallways. They can showcase any topic: famous inventions, Spanish culture, witchcraft, King Minos's labyrinth, the whaling industry, the interior of the human heart.

Begin by designing the exploratorium on paper. Then erect the walls and mold the spaces using such material as tin foil, sheets, tri-wall, refrigerator boxes, packing crates, and giant cardboard tubes. Complex exploratoriums require teamwork for their construction. Break the class into small groups and have each group work on a particular area and its contents: pictures, sculpture, super-8 movies, prerecorded audiotapes, and so forth. Remind students about lighting effects, including color, blinking, and angling. After you've put the exploratorium together, invite other classes to lose themselves in it.

The Board Game

Many games are played with designed objects: boards, cards, and "pieces." Whether the design at hand is as simple as a checkerboard or as complex as a Monopoly board, it is usually intrinsic to the way the game is actually played, and not merely decorative.

When your students begin thinking up ideas for board games, make sure they don't sacrifice excitement for ostensible instructional value. Too many commercially produced "educational games" are not so much games as contests, won by spelling words correctly, solving arithmetic problems, or recalling history facts. Instead of simply tapping rote knowledge, games ought to involve kids in analysis, strategy, and other mental skills.

Almost any curricular issue may be developed into a board game (and many of them already have been by commercial companies): politics, perception, economics, art history. At the elementary level, the classic, endlessly variable "Uncle Wiggily" format—spin the pointer, move the appropriate number of spaces, hope to get there first—is particularly serviceable. Older kids can invent games in which tactics are as decisive as fortune.°

Standards

Most of the media we discuss in this book are like magnets. What kid can resist snapping a Polaroid photograph or recording his voice on tape? But drawing is different. The majority of students soon come to believe that they can't draw. As long as they believe this, they won't.°

Most students believe that they can't draw. As long as they believe this, they won't.

Thus, defeatism is the first "error" you may have to overcome in teaching through design. To put it more positively: build confidence. One strategy is to have your students draw for younger children. Projects can range from coloring books to cartoons. Another approach is for kids to keep portfolios of their drawings, just as they keep folders of their writings. This will get them competing with themselves, not with the class's champion drawers. Once the volume of design reaches a respectable flow, students should watch out for such common problems as:

Limp Lines. Drawing competence begins with the ability to make strong, bold, outspoken lines. Some common scribble and doodle exercises can help students to overcome drawing diffidence.

1. Take one of your favorite verbs—splash, zoom, jump, dance, sparkle, fly, explode—and express it in a few spontaneous sweeps of your pencil or pen.

2. Listen to a variety of musical selections—jazz, rock, blues, classical—and try to show what you hear in clear, unhesitant strokes.

3. Without lifting your pencil or pen off the paper, draw an irregular line—one with curves or bumps or angles—from one edge to the other. Now draw twenty or thirty additional lines, all of them following your first line very closely without touching or crossing it. The more lines you add paralleling your original, the more you will find fascinating shapes and patterns swelling up on your page.

Premature Detail. Students should get the overall pattern of their pictures down before they start fussing over details. If a kid is making a drawing of a hand, for example, adding every fingernail or palm line will not coax it into looking like a hand if the basic contours are wrong. Better to start over.

Faulty Proportions. Children love to draw people, but often they end up with monsters—misshapen individuals sporting shrunken heads, elephantine legs, and arms ending abruptly at the waist. What's unsatisfying about these pictures is not the elements themselves but the size relationships among those elements. One help is for students to memorize certain basic proportional facts about the human body. Arms, for example, extend to mid-thigh. (The tendency is to make them shorter.) Eyes are practically in the middle of the head. (The tendency is to make them higher.) A hand can almost cover its owner's face. (The tendency is to make it smaller.) Another trick, useful when drawing complicated images containing several different subjects, is to select a single detail—a chair, a door, a human head—and use it as a mental "yardstick" for determining the relative sizes of everything else. A third approach to proportion consciousness is for students to use faulty size relationships intentionally, making "caricature" drawings in which a famous or fictional individual's most striking feature—nose, eyes, chin, hair, waistline—is greatly exaggerated.

Underdone Overlapping. Overlapping, in which an object hides part of another object from view, enables an artist to achieve convincing, dramatic results. Hats snuggle down over heads instead of just balancing on them; noses cease simply to decorate faces and start to sprout in three-dimensional splendor; graveyards come alive with real, solid tombstones. As soon as they are old enough to understand the meaning of the word (and before, if possible), students should try to add overlapping to their drawing skills. But be sure they don't use the technique halfheartedly. An overlapping object should cover a substantial portion of the object "behind" it (see the *Concepts* section). Otherwise, the artist may get what professionals call a "bad tangent," wherein a *single* line seems to define and belong to two *different* objects. Such ambiguous ownership leads to an ambiguous image.

Unerased Irrelevancies. Every amateur knows the aggravation of getting basic contour lines in the wrong place, sketching in details that later look pointless, drawing elements way out of proportion, forgetting to leave out the hidden parts of an overlapped object, and, of course, making a succession of false starts. There's no shame in any of this; accomplished illustrators fall prey to the same problems. All that's needed is to activate the other end of the pencil. A typical drawing session is a continual give-and-take between rubber and graphite, with the artist unconsciously flipping her pencil back and forth like a baton.

Stereotyped Solutions. Everyone, even a child, knows that a turkey doesn't really look like an outline of a human hand, that the sun doesn't really look like a pincushion, and that a tree doesn't really look like a lollipop. Yet teachers often encourage children to adopt these ready-made images, perhaps because they know such solutions are fool-proof and convenient, perhaps because they feel classroom "art" can never rise above the lollipop level anyway. As early as possible, kids should understand the legitimacy of sketching from real-life models. Fantasy pictures of demons, dragons, and unknown worlds are equally valid, of course, but when the need to draw something commonplace arises—a flower, a fish, a flag—the best source of inspiration is not imagination or formulas, but actual flowers, fish, and flags.

Finally, plan to be supportive during the long periods of frustration that any design novice will encounter. The struggle, in Jules Feiffer's words, goes something like this: "It happened in spurts. Nothing for a while: not being able to catch on, not being able to foreshorten correctly, or get perspectives straight or get the blacks to look right. Then suddenly: a breakthrough. One morning you can draw forty percent better than you could when you quit the night before. Then, again, you coast. Your critical abilities improve but your talent won't. Nothing works. Despair. Then another breakthrough. Magically, it keeps happening. Soon it stops being magic, just becomes education."

Sources and Resources

1. The Feiffer comments here and at the end of the chapter appear in his introduction to *The Great Comic Book Heroes* (New York: Bonanza Books, imprint of Crown Publishers, 1965).

2. Bruce McIntyre's books include *Drawing Textbook, Best Book on Drawing People*, and *Big Easel II*, all available from The Audio-Visual Drawing Program, 1014 North Wright Street, Santa Ana, CA 92701. A witty programmed-learning course in cartoon illustration, similar to the McIntyre system, is *The Big Yellow Drawing Book* (Nevada City, CA: Hugh O'Neill and Associates, 1974).

3. An inspiring book on cartooning, based on the experiences of real-world artists, is Nick Meglin's *The Art of Humorous Illustration* (New York: Watson-Guptill Publications, 1973).

4. Reproductions of the first *Superman, Batman, Wonder Woman,* and *Captain Marvel* adventures are available from National Periodical Publications, 75 Rockefeller Plaza, New York, NY 10016. Although the comic established itself through assorted caped crusaders, the best quality, wittiest, most imaginative comic book stories are generally found in other, non-superhero genres. If Batman is not

your students' cup of tea, try showing them *The Spirit, Tintin* (a French series), *Uncle Scrooge*, and EC Science Fiction. The Spirit's exploits are presently being reprinted by Warren Publishing Company, 145 East 32nd Street, New York, NY 10016. Tintin's adventures, both hardbound and softbound, are becoming increasingly available in American book stores. *Uncle Scrooge* reprints occasionally appear on a newsstand or in a supermarket. EC Science Fiction comics like *Weird Fantasy* and *Weird Science* are available from East Coast Comics, 3599 Swenson Street, Las Vegas, NV 89109.

5. Edward De Bono's diagram books are published by Simon and Schuster, New York.

6. For a straightforward, well-written analysis of basic board game categories, see *A Player's Guide to Table Games* by John Jackson (Harrisburg, PA: Stackpole Books).

7. A dandy little book for people who "can't draw a straight line" is Barbara Cram Gilmore's *Instant Talent* (Rutland, VT: Charles E. Tuttle Company, 1967).

PROFESSOR MINDBOGGLE *tells* HOW TO MAKE COMICS

BY JIM MORROW & RON HARRIS

CLIFF AND ARNIE! WHAT ARE YOU UP TO?

WE WANT TO LEARN HOW TO MAKE COMIC BOOKS, PROFESSOR MINDBOGGLE.

WELL, FIRST YOU TAKE A PENCIL AND A RULER AND DRAW THE BOXES WHERE THE PICTURES GO.

THESE BOXES ARE CALLED **PANELS.** MOST COMICS HAVE SIX OR EIGHT PANELS ON EACH PAGE!

MAYBE YOU NEVER THOUGHT ABOUT IT, BUT YOU HAVE TO LEARN TO READ COMICS JUST AS YOU HAVE TO LEARN TO READ REGULAR BOOKS.

YOU READ A BOOK FROM LEFT TO RIGHT — IT'S THE SAME WITH COMICS!

AND YOU ALWAYS GO FROM THE TOP...

...TO THE BOTTOM!

SOMETIMES YOU'LL WANT TO DRAW **ARROWS** TO SHOW PEOPLE THE **ORDER** OF THE PANELS!

Print: 5
Playing the wild card medium

"I had gone on the assumption that 2,000 to 3,000 words a day was a writer's proper stint, perhaps the maximum one is capable of. . . . But to meet *The Shadow* schedule I had to hit 5,000 words or more per day. I geared for that pace and found that instead of being worn out by 5,000 words I was just reaching my peak. . . . By living, thinking, even dreaming the story in one continuous process, ideas came faster and faster. Sometimes the typewriter keys would fly so fast that I wondered if my fingers could keep up with them. At the finish of the story I often had to take a few days off as my fingertips were too sore to begin on the next book."°

The speaker is Walter Brown Gibson, a pulp magazine employee who once specialized in *The Shadow*. As a model of print-in-action, Gibson's writing may seem a peculiar choice. Surely pulp magazines have little to do with formal education, and surely their practitioners are not "real writers" in the sense of Goethe or Hemingway or even Agatha Christie.

And yet the Gibsons of the writing world count for something. Their prose is not great, but it is not awful either. *Shadow* pulps contain few grammatical errors, a varied vocabulary, a vigorous style, and occasionally even a memorable image: "Unseen lips produced a peal of sudden mirth—a strange, shuddering mockery, like a whisper that had come to life." What teacher would not like to make the same claim for her students' papers?

Gibson knew that the only way to learn writing is to write a lot. To get the words flowing, you must cycle your thoughts directly from your brain to your fingers to your paper and back again. Gibson did not write carelessly or unconsciously. He did not even write "spontaneously." But he did write freely, and he did his thinking while he was writing.

Many kids, of course, have trouble thinking on paper. One solution is to get them thinking and composing out loud—in the oral tradition discussed in the Stage chapter. Before a student attempts to write an essay or short story or review, suggest he or she talk the subject over with a friend, or with several friends at different times. Settling on ideas—and even shaping phrases—out loud is a good way to prime the pencil. (Cheap cassette tape recorders, so worthless for sound production per se, are a real help in this kind of activity.) True, writing involves many idioms, conventions, and potentialities not inherent in speech. But an approach that links pencil to tongue will convince kids that they already possess the basic vocabulary and grammar tools and will make novices feel less like aliens in the world of print.

Concepts

Teaching the similarities between speaking and writing can give kids the heart to write. Teaching them the differences can give them the craft.

When we talk with someone or some group, it's not hard to tell if our message is getting through. And should we choose, we can put the feedback—laughter, puzzled stares, verbal asides—to immediate use by changing our message to overcome problems or exploit successes.

How different with print. Here the message is completed before the audience receives it. Usually the writer is not there. He may live in a distant place. He may be dead. He cannot rely upon his intended audience for help in perfecting his message, which means he must do his trial-and-erring before the moment of communication. This process revolves around four issues: idea, wording, editing, and publishing.

Idea

In any writing activity, the kernel idea usually includes not only a *what* component—what the idea is—but also a *how* component. The treatment of the idea is, in fact, part of the idea itself. Thus, the idea for the novel *Frankenstein* is not simply "a scientist creates an artificial man" but, as Mary Shelley has made clear in several autobiographical notes, "the classic Prometheus plot done up as a Gothic horror story." The idea for Howard Koch's script of the famous Orson Welles radio drama, *Invasion from*

Beginning writers are not plagiarizing if they base a piece of writing on someone else's idea.

Mars, is not simply "an adaptation of H. G. Wells's *The War of the Worlds*," but "*The War of the Worlds* treated as a series of up-to-the-minute radio news bulletins."

The writer's main job is to take the idea and write it out, turning it into a finished print production. In other words, the writer is not necessarily the person who comes up with the idea in the first place. It was director Welles, not writer Koch, who hit upon composing the *Invasion from Mars* script from news flashes, and many magazine articles are thought up by editors and "assigned" to staff writers. Thus, while it is commendable for beginning writers to avoid plagiarism like the plague, they are not plagiarizing if they base a piece of writing on someone else's idea, provided they acknowledge the source and take credit only for the execution.

The treatment part of any writing idea includes at least five elements.

Format. The choices are intoxicating: novel, short story, metered poem, free-verse poem, one-act play, song lyric, movie review, advertising copy, editorial, biography, autobiography. And, of course, the "non-print" projects discussed in this book—comics,

photo essays, slide-tapes, films, TV shows—often require written scripts.

Point. What will the finished work accomplish? In the classroom, the point is usually to display recently acquired knowledge to the teacher. In real-world writing, the range is much broader—to tickle, soothe, upset, convince, puzzle, support, convulse, stimulate, impress, terrify. The simple act of applying a stated goal to the format he has chosen (a funny essay, for example) can invigorate an amateur's writing.

Length. In the classroom, a common question is, "How long should the paper be?" The teacher is outraged, believing that students should always think in terms of quality rather than quantity.

But the length question is valid. In the real world, a writer's editor tells him how many words the assignment is "worth"—a balance of probable reader interest, complexity of idea, and economics (available space). The concept also applies to works not written expressly for publication. For example, a poet might be gripped by the idea of a very short poem on the fate of the American Indian, capturing the tragedy in a few telling verses; or he may decide that only an extremely lengthy poem, a true "American epic," can give the subject its due.

Slant. Consciously or unconsciously, all writers slant the concepts, vocabulary, and style of their productions toward an intended audience. A story may receive a happy ending for no reason other than the author's conviction that his readers want one. Slanting is not dishonest. It is the act of considering the audience. Every writer must master this process, learning, say, the difference between writing for a business executive and a college freshman.

Point of View. Every good writer knows the power of "voice." In one of his stories, for example, Franz Kafka explores the irrationality of divine omnipotence by assuming the perspective of a dog. Melville begins *Moby Dick* by involving the reader directly ("Call me Ishmael"), moving immediately to a conventional first person viewpoint ("Some years ago . . . I thought I would sail about a little and see the watery part of the world"), detaching the narrator's ego from events and making him part of a group ("It must be borne in mind that all this time we have a Sperm Whale's prodigious head hanging to the Pequod's side"), and, finally, returning to his narrator's individual experiences ("Buoyed up by that coffin, for almost one whole day and night, I floated on a soft and dirge-like main").

Wording

English textbooks often talk about "word attack" skills, as if words were an enemy to be beaten into

THE SCIENCE FICTION HORROR MOVIE POCKET COMPUTER
by
Gahan Wilson

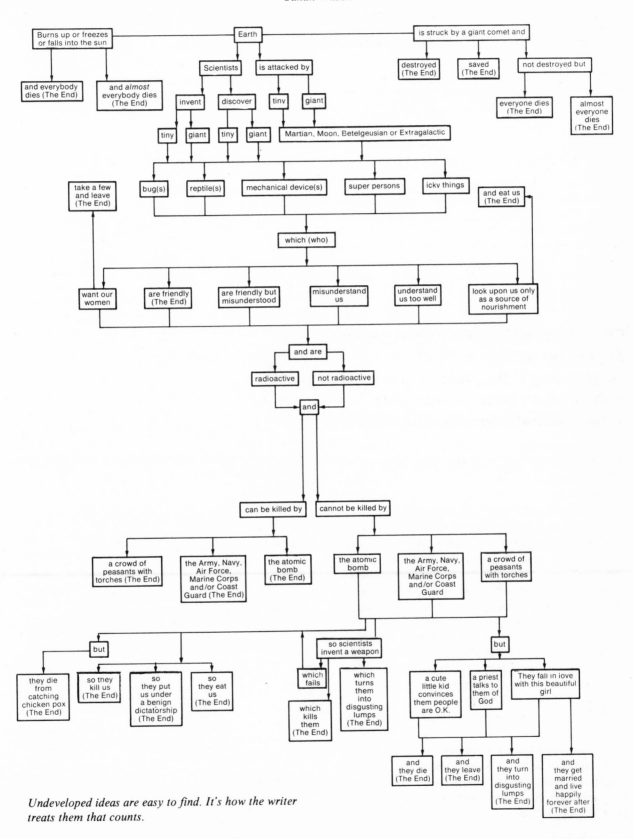

Undeveloped ideas are easy to find. It's how the writer treats them that counts.

In print production, writing and editing are different skills.

submission. But professional writers take a more loving attitude. They romance words, play games with them, and put them into elegant arrangements.

One classic approach to wording consciousness is harvesting memorable turns of phrase as they occur in casual conversation, the natural environment, or your own thoughts. We know several do-it-yourself Bartletteers who carry three-by-five cards or phrase-collection notebooks with them at all times. Among our own recent acquisitions are "a lame buck administration" and "opening up a can of words."

Phrase-makers start not with rules but with full-grown ideas, getting the wording right in a single deft stroke of pen or tongue. An adage of comedy writing holds that the first way you think to phrase a joke is usually the best way. Occasionally, however, an author will have an inspired idea for a line, but what he's put down just doesn't work. That's the time for him to ask questions about the order, choice, and quantity of his words.

Order. Robert Ardrey's 1961 book, *African Genesis*, begins with the line, "Not in innocence, and not in Asia, was mankind born." A more conventional ordering would have been "Mankind was born neither in innocence nor in Asia." By beginning on the word "not" and holding his surprise twist for the last—most English sentences don't end on the verb—Ardrey fires his controversial thesis with audacity and drama.

Choice. Sometimes a strong word is all that's needed to make a phrase. Mark Twain once wrote, "Loyalty to petrified opinion never yet broke a chain or freed a human soul." "Never yet" is right here, easily eclipsing a variation like "hardly ever" or "rarely ever." At other times, understatement is required. Twain also said, "Reports of my death are greatly exaggerated." "Exaggerated" is the key. A less equivocal version like "Reports of my death are false" misses the mark.

Quantity. The words in a good line are pared to an optimum. Thus, Ambrose Bierce defines "prejudice" as "a vagrant opinion without visible means of support" rather than as "a vagrant opinion that doesn't have any visible means of support." Occasionally, however, one must *add* words to get the rhythm right. For most people, "These are the times that try men's souls" rings truer than "These times try men's souls."

Editing

In print production, writing and editing are different skills. The right person to draft a particular magazine article, short story, book review, or novel is not necessarily the right person to pound it into final shape. Writers need a talent for inspiration, ideas, and felicitous wording. Editors need a talent for cutting, transposing, and proofing.

Cutting. One way to discover whether a piece of prose is overwritten is to lop off the first paragraph. Often the piece will not only make just as much sense, it will now boast a more intriguing beginning.

Besides this kind of radical surgery, editors must also weigh the aptness of each individual word. Sometimes the word is obvious and should be replaced by something more imaginative, as when editor Eugene Field turned "He played King Lear unenthusiastically" into "He played King Lear as though someone had led the ace." Sometimes the word is inaccurate or imprecise, as when a writer uses "electric" for "electronic." And sometimes the word simply has no business being there, as when "I know the reason why he died" is used instead of the equally clear "I know why he died," or when we are told that something is "highly unique" or "in close proximity."

Transposing. Editors are forever rearranging the order of paragraphs and the order of sentences within those paragraphs, all the while keeping the sense intact through an occasional skillful word change. This process can clarify the author's meaning, flush out unnecessary passages, and make the piece "track" so effortlessly that the reader never stumbles.

Proofing. All successful writers have taken the trouble to master standard grammar, which puts them in a position to opt for phrasing that sounds right even though it is technically incorrect. Guided by her image of the intended reader and by the policies of her periodical or publishing house, the editor will decide whether to accept an appropriate sentence fragment, split infinitive, "who" for "whom," preposition before a period, sentence beginning with "And," or common expression like "It's me." Spelling, punctuation, typographical, and even subject-verb agreement errors will occasionally haunt the work of even the most accomplished author, and the editor must see that these are proofread out of town.

Publishing

Publishing makes the writing effort real. Two major dimensions of publishing are circulation and visualization.

Circulation. For the first time in history, print is becoming a mass medium not just in its reactive phase, reading, but in its active phase, writing. Electrostatic copiers (such as the Xerox machine) and modern offset techniques enable all print practitioners to achieve a "circulation." College towns in particular offer these duplicating methods at reasonably low prices (three cents per copy as of this writing). With small runs (fewer than fifty copies of each page) offset is usually more expensive than xerography, but many amateurs are willing to pay for it anyway. There is something sterile about the grays of most present xerography, whereas with offset one gets the classic effect of dark black ink printed on paper, a bold, powerful contrast which tells the reader that these words matter.

Visualization. Even if his work is not duplicated, a good writer gives careful consideration to the visual appearance of the final draft. Some relevant questions: Should a special style of type be selected for the title, chapter names, or subheads? Should the text be supplemented with photographs or illustrations? Should there be a cover? Should the manuscript be typed or should it be hand-written?

To achieve perfect-looking final drafts, professionals often use white opaquing fluid to cover over typing or handwriting errors. This inexpensive trick-of-the-trade can encourage novices to be extra careful in proofreading their manuscripts. They'll know they won't have to redo an entire page just to fix up one small mistake. The most reliable brand is called "Liquid Paper Correction Fluid."°

Activities

The expression "creative writing" is common only in schools. Real-world writers know that it does not necessarily require more creativity to produce a great short story than a great magazine feature. A copywriter creating a fifteen-word advertisement may need the ear of a Haiku poet. The challenge of writing is offered not by format but by that frightening object, the blank piece of paper.

We hope that the following eight activities are more provocative than frightening. They should give children experience with point of view, editing, word choice, and other concepts discussed above. We've discovered that most of these activities can be handled as either fiction or nonfiction. Thus, students can publish a newspaper about the discovery of life on Uranus, or a song lyric about a historical figure.

the sun is our model of a loving consciousness. enlightenment is a sunny disposition. the more you relax, the more loving your consciousness becomes, until it shines through all acquired conditioning and you are as radiant as the sun.

gazing at sunlight is relaxing & quieting to the mind. living in nature, away from civilization, in a sunny place is the simple road to bliss. (see warning on page 200)
12

Typesetting is not essential for professional-looking books, as shown by this excerpt from Being of the Sun *(Harper and Row).*

```
Zontar:  The Thing From Venus (1965)

     I seem to remember someone saying that Curse
of the Swamp Creature was John Agar's worst movie
(or anyone's for that matter).  Even so, this film has
to come as a close second.  Made by the same people as
Curse, this film has a script and cast that would be
all too easily forgotten.  A remake of the already rotten
It Conquered the World, the villain is actually a rubber
suited beast with no recognizable features.  It looks
something like a blob of putty with rubber wings attached.
Zontar takes over people's minds and turns them into
cold-blooded zombies, according to the story.  Now, take
this in mind.  The rest of the cast are not supposed to
be zombies.  That's pretty hard to believe, once you see
their acting abilities.  In the end, the hero shoots
all the zombies, who die in a ridiculously amateurish
manner, and saves the world.  As is often found in these
sort of films, an optimistic speech is rendered at the
end.  This time, however, they surpass themselves by
stating that man is the greatest creature in the universe.
The fact that this speech is given over the pictures of
mutilated corpses, makes one wonder if the filmmaker
himself believes in these naive ideals.

                              -- Eric Stanway
```

Movie review by Eric Stanway, age 15.

The Review

Reviewing someone else's work is one of the best ways to express your own personality, prejudices, or knowledge. This is not dreary, name-of-my-book stuff but a hearty, heady assignment. Yet as the movie review by a junior high student on this page shows, the task is well within the reach of young people.

Whether they are evaluating films, plays, books, restaurants, concerts, or political speeches, kids should be aware of the following elements common to most professional reviews:

Gut Reaction. Typically, a review takes off from the writer's subjective response to the work—liking or hating or being bored by it. Note in the *Zontar* critique how Stanway announces his personal feelings by relating the film to a notorious effort (*Curse of the Swamp Creature*) he once heard about. Another technique is for the reviewer to contrast his general biases with his immediate reaction: "I ordinarily loathe Italian food, but the ravioli at Antonio's Pizza Parlor is. . . ." Finally, the reader may objectify his gut response by describing how the production went over with the rest of the audience.

Description. Reviews often include a word-picture of the work. With narratives—plays, novels, television series, and movies—this overview may be a plot summary. (Too many students and TV news commentators, unfortunately, never learn that such summarizing is merely a prelude to the hard work of reviewing.) The descriptive element in reviewing nonnarrative subjects like food or cars is a greater challenge, but it can provoke colorful, precise writing.

Analysis. Comments like "It was a beautiful film" or "The band was awful" tell very little. The analytic process moves a review beyond generalization and pinpoints particular problems the creator solved or failed to solve. Stanway, for example, attacks *Zontar* by singling out scripting, acting, and costuming.

Background Information. Background information can help people to see a work in new ways and even modify their gut reactions. Here's a chance for applied research. For example, once you inform an audience that Orson Welles's second film, *The Magnificent Ambersons*, was butchered by the studio in the editing room and given an ending he never wanted, they may rank Welles's accomplishments in this picture much higher.

Consumer Advice. One summation technique is to tell the reader whether he should experience the work himself: "If you're been having trouble falling asleep lately, tune in the Jack Freebush show."

Critics can seem like negative souls, but this is rarely a matter of personality. It is simply that there are more bad works than good ones. For the student reviewer this reality is an asset since it's easier (and more fun) to rip a bad work than praise a good one.

While the review's place in literature classes is obvious, the format can get a student dealing dynamically with any discipline's instructional materials. Have kids write about commercially produced textbooks, filmstrips, and movies, as well as documentary specials on TV. They can share their best reviews with other teachers, with the materials purchasing committee, and with the materials producers themselves. Fictional reviews are another rich possibility. This approach enables the student to conceive of epic poems, ten-hour movies, and encyclopedic novels without actually having to create them.

The Letter

Because there's nothing like instant feedback, the telephone has taken over much of the long-distance communication once accomplished by letter. Still, the format has its virtues. Letters are cheap, tangible, and reproducible. Many people, especially the high and mighty, are difficult to reach by phone, but they or their representatives will usually answer mail. Letters can be both a mass medium, as when they are published in a newspaper or tacked to a bulletin board, and a "reverse mass medium," as when hundreds or even thousands of people petition a single party. (Try doing *that* over the telephone!)

Letter writing is perhaps the only kind of discourse to use the I-thou point of view unselfconsciously, and it can provide a merry change from the disembodied prose of assignments patterned after (or cribbed from) encyclopedia articles. Unfortunately, the me-to-youness of letter-writing is often lost in schools amid exercises that teach the difference between "business" and "friendly" letters, as if business letters can't be friendly and letters to friends can't handle business. Worse, classroom letter writing is often introduced as an *en masse* project— "Let's all write to the President telling him how to fix up the country." It's hard to imagine an exercise better designed to foil the intimacy of letters. You might as well have kids play group chess.

To put students in touch with the personal nature of the format, have them try "the fictional letter." This genre, rarely explored in schools, enables the writer to tell a story or make a point by taking both sides in an exchange. Kids can write letters that might have been sent between historical contemporaries (Anthony and Cleopatra, Michelangelo and Leonardo da Vinci) or between people of different

periods (Newton and Einstein, Schubert and Schönberg). The correspondents can themselves be fictional: letters between Hamlet and Lord Jim or even between characters out of the student's imagination.

Naturally, opportunities for nonfiction correspondence will arise during the year. Letters can be used to ferret out live information on any topic. Maybe the student disagrees with a point in the textbook and wants to tell the author about it. Perhaps someone really has something to say to the President. Nonfiction letters enable kids to exercise their freedom of speech by writing to local, state, or federal officials, and to exercise their powers of analysis by picking apart the pre-printed replies they get back. These are all authentic moments for drafting formally correct letters. But it will be up to the writer to decide whether the letter should be friendly or not.

The Instruction Manual

A bonus of the instructional manual format is that it gives students objective feedback on their ability to write clearly. Either the reader correctly slips plug A into socket B, thereby activating his new electric can opener, or he is misled and plugs A into X, thereby blowing up his side of the street. Here are step-by-step directions for introducing this activity to a class. Be sure to follow them carefully.

1. Ask each child to write instructions for tying a shoelace, playing tic-tac-toe, or any other simple endeavor.
2. As one student reads his or her directions aloud, have another carry them out literally. (The results will usually be hilarious as well as educational.)
3. Discuss problems caused by poor word choice, illogical sequencing, and insufficient detail.
4. Show kids examples of well-done or poorly done instructions for games, model kits, and household appliances.
5. Later, suggest that students produce instruction manuals as projects in science (how to grow crystals, how to make a garden, how to use a bunsen burner); geography (how to get from the school to the firehouse); physical education (how to play volleyball, how to do yoga); home economics (a recipe for shortbread); or social studies (rules of behavior—laws, manners, rituals).

The Song Lyric

If you travel around the country listening to the radio, you may discover that a melody used to sell spaghetti in your hometown accompanies lyrics

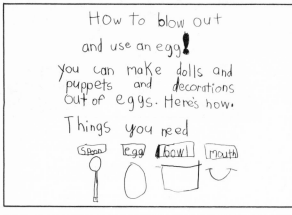

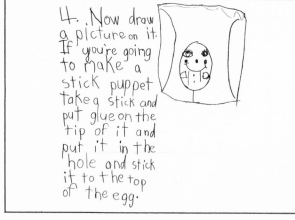

Instructions dictated and then copied by Anna Lisa Suid, age 6. Note the use of a narrative introduction and steps keyed to clarifying illustrations.

about a used-car dealership somewhere else. It's surprising how a tune having no intended relationship with a particular set of lyrics can still seem to belong to them. This can happen even if the melody is familiar, as when in the 1964 presidential campaign, Lyndon Johnson's staff used "Hello Dolly" to get people singing "Hello, Lyndon."

Many historic songs were born this way. For example, Samuel Smith wrote the hymn "America" to the tune of the Prussian national song (not knowing the British had borrowed it, too). Even Broadway is not above such piggy-backing; the musical *Kismet* took all its music from the works of the Russian composer, Borodin.

These examples imply that students can become lyricists without possessing a talent for melody-making. They can start with old-time favorites, pop songs, movie themes, or classical music. For beginners, though, suggest very straightforward tunes—"Clementine," "For He's a Jolly Good Fellow," "The Battle Hymn of the Republic."

Like professional lyricists, kids can write songs about any topic, including curricular matters. Tom Lehrer's hilarious but instructive song about "The Elements," for instance, was written to the tune of Gilbert and Sullivan's "I Am the Very Model of a Modern Major General." Students can also incorporate their lyrics into other media formats—slide-tapes, comic books, puppet shows, TV variety acts.

The Children's Book

After years of composing for well-informed, highly literate adults, older students may find writing for young children a refreshing, low-pressure activity. This is not to say it is childish. Children's literature touches basic human concerns, from birth to death, fear to love, art to animality. All the devices vital to adult writing—metaphor, irony, punning, dialogue, overstatement, understatement—also work for children.

To convince a student that the children's book is a challenging format, have him read classic examples—fiction, nonfiction, prose, poetry—to a little kid. Actual projects can originate in several ways. Perhaps a kindergarten or first grade teacher will solicit works on issues of relevance to her charges: a history of the school, a bit of nonsense phonics ("the fox ate the box/the box ate the fox"), a rhyming number-facts book. Or you might advise your students that producing a children's book will fulfill a fiction writing assignment.

By far the richest possibility, from the standpoint of covering subject matter, is to have students create children's books on whatever topic they themselves are studying—Abe Lincoln, how bees communicate,

Few efforts bring a person in closer touch with a subject than trying to present it clearly and honestly to children.

the American Indian. Few efforts bring a person in closer touch with a subject than trying to present it clearly and honestly to children. Your kids will find they cannot translate the material until they have mastered it themselves. After selecting an idea, the student can move through the following sequence:

Work up a treatment. This might include an outline, a projected length in words or pages, and a statement of whether the text will be in prose or poetry.

Write a first draft. If the book is nonfiction—the history of dinosaurs, for example—this step will likely involve library research.

Read the draft. The student writer should test out his draft on a sample child or two and revise it accordingly.

Create the illustrations. This involves figuring out where illustrations should go in relation to the text; choosing the media (drawings, photos of live subjects, photos of models, or even three-dimensional cut-outs or objects pasted onto the pages); and executing the art work. Your students may wish to follow the popular real-world practice of teaming an illustrator with a writer.

Set the type. The text can be hand-printed or typed. Important words can be cut out of magazines or created with rub-on letters.

Combine art and type. Some students will wish to attach the pictures to the pages of finished type; others will wish to paste the type onto the illustrations.

Bind the book. Among the methods are sewing, stapling, clamping, and ring binding. Whichever method he chooses, the student should create a catchy cover since, while you can't *tell* a book by its cover, you can *sell* one that way.°

The Script

In a multi-media culture, script writing is a most important use of print. Since each medium has special requirements—a radio script is very different from a movie script—we've presented models and tips in appropriate places throughout the book.

But we want to include "the script" here for three reasons. First, kids may wish to throw their creative souls into scripts they can't possibly produce. Even

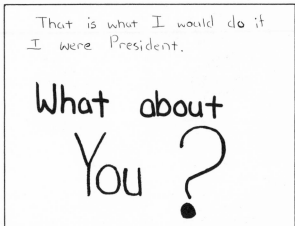

Excerpts from a children's book, If I Were President, *created by Amy Chang, age 10.*

without an "angel," a student can have fun concocting mighty epic films or dazzling musical comedies. By the same token, kids can create modest one-act plays that work so well on paper there is no point (and maybe even some risk) in handing them over to the drama club.

Finally, and most important, there is a species of script that is in fact meant only to be read, never produced. Such scripts are generally based on conversation, often intermixed with wonderfully absurd stage directions. This format can be used for reporting actual exchanges (an argument between two kids on the playground), for speculating on historic events (what Columbus said to convince Isabella to fund his voyages), or to personify concepts and objects (a debate between my id and my superego, or a discussion between an equilateral and an isosceles triangle about the shape of things).

The Newspaper

The modern newspaper subsumes over a dozen print formats. These include: the chronicle (news stories), the essay (editorials, columns, reviews), the biography (obituaries), the instruction (how-to-do-it features on gardening, photography, romance), the crossword puzzle, the letter, the wit-twister, the joke, the caption, the horoscope, even the dialogue (comic strips). A typical daily is a correspondence school offering courses in science, politics, psychology, the arts, ethics, economics, and technology.

The applications of newspaper production to the curriculum are plentiful. "One-shot" editions can dramatize an important day in history, a kind of print version of "You Are There." A student newspaper dated July 4, 1776 might feature straight news items on the signing of the Declaration, profiles of major participants, and pro and con reactions expressed in letters to the editor. Cartoons, jokes, and features on bread-baking or candle-making could further establish the character of the time.

This activity can also help kids organize their insights into works of fiction—a front page based on Hecht and MacArthur's *The Front Page*, or an "extra" about the murder of Caesar based on a reading of Shakespeare. In a foreign language class, a student might put out a paper by translating a real-world daily or, better still, fabricating news stories from his imagination. Kids can use this format for prediction by producing a newspaper from the year 3000, complete with advertisements for new products and editorials dealing with the possible concerns of their progeny.

Whatever its aim, the ultimate challenge of making a classroom newspaper is getting it to look real.

Newspaper by Audrey Bryant, age 11. This authentic-looking layout, submitted as a social studies project, incorporates such real-world newspaper elements as a flag *("The Old Chronicle"), a* caption *("New whaling ship"),* headlines *("Whaling Comes to California"),* bylines *("By Joe Smith"),* jumplines *("continued on page 3"),* column dividing lines, *a* box, *an* illustration, *plus a variety of print sizes and weights (the headlines are larger and darker than the story text).*

Most of the fun and educational value will be lost if the product resembles the school's dittoed-in-blue daily bulletin. The annotated front page opposite suggests the visual elements to keep in mind.

The Magazine

At the core of every successful magazine is a unifying concept, often stated in its title: *Psychology Today, The New York Times Book Review, Mad, Model Railroader, Reader's Digest, Film Quarterly, Business Week, Skin Diver, Consumer Reports, The English Journal, The Creature Gazette.* Magazines like these generally reflect the interests or worldview of a minority. Thus, the format can play a role in "individualized" education as students, working alone or in like-minded coteries, bring out publications devoted to rock music, sports, flying saucers, cooking, or do-it-yourself electronics.

Since every discipline breaks into specialties, you can further individualize learning by co-publishing with your students a variety of unstuffy scholarly magazines. In history, for example, consider inventing a periodical that explores the past through such fascinating items as stamps, maps, songs, photos of artifacts discovered in antique stores, and reviews of historical films. In an English class focused on poetry or story writing, magazines become an excellent way to showcase work, inspire careful editing, and boost morale. Kids will come up with anything from the traditional literary journal to pulp magazines full of intentional melodramatics.

In the next column are some highlights from the third issue of *The Creature Gazette*, a horror movie "fanzine" created by several junior high kids. We include it not as a format model—your students should survey the range, from basically all-print journals like *Reader's Digest* to heavily pictorial magazines like *Sports Illustrated*—but simply because it proves so eloquently that students can be as lively with magazine-making as with any other media activity.

One particularly dynamic component of almost all magazines is "the advertisement." If you doubt the educational value of writing ad copy, think back to the times when all you had to do was explain in twenty-five words or less why Zopps was the best soap (cereal, soda) you ever washed with (ate, drank). The grand prize might have been an all-expense-paid vacation on the Riviera or possibly an all-expense-paid life. But even if you didn't win the big one, there were always 50,000 other fantastic prizes.

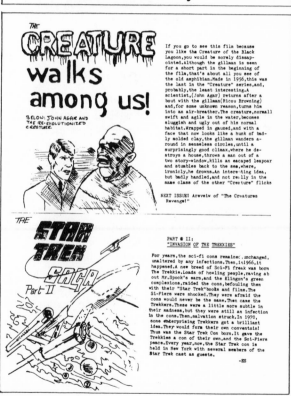

The Creature Gazette *is published irregularly by five teenagers: Eric Stanway (editor and founder), Peter Reynolds (co-editor and circulation specialist), Phil Stanway (layout and assistant editor), Paul Reynolds (technical assistant), and Sean Tracy (foreign correspondent).*

We never actually met anyone who won anything by writing those twenty-five words (or less), but the task did teach us a lot about word-choice, brevity, slanting, punning, and using humor to get a point across. Surely it can do the same for your kids. With so few words expected, the task won't overwhelm the reluctant writer. On the other hand, students who run off at the pen will face the challenge of making every word count. Finally, copywriting is a happy way to practice punctuation. While ads don't require lots of punctuation, what's there has got to be right. A well-placed ellipsis (. . .) or question mark can make all the difference. Period.

Of the many types of ads, the one that seems to work best with kids is the classic Volkswagen format: a single, often provocative picture with a relatively brief but also provocative—or even cryptic—caption. A trailing paragraph or two illuminates both picture and caption.

Students can use ads to promote anything from the first abacus (in a math journal) to a play by Molière (dans une revue française). In a *Time*-like publication, current events may inspire ads—for instance, an ad for a country seeking foreign investments or an ad by a political candidate. A magazine about health could feature ads taking opposite sides of issues like smoking, jogging, or meat-eating.

Standards

At every level of education, teachers complain that their students' writing is ungrammatical, illogical, messy, dull, and pointless. Serious as this situation is, it would be a complete catastrophe only if kids themselves were ungrammatical, illogical, messy, dull, and pointless.

While it's true that many kids fumble conventional usage in their writing and can profit from an occasional lesson in punctuation or agreement, we believe that the real root of their print problems is that they are forced to work alone. It is considered "cheating" for students to receive aid and comfort from friends, relatives, writing experts, or models in the culture at large. Yet nothing could be further from real-world practice.

Check out the acknowledgments in most books and you'll see how social the print medium really is. Writers are not being modest when they share the glory with editors, friends, colleagues, researchers, spouses, typists, and others who helped nurture the project from brainstorm to royalty check. Professional writers need this kind of assistance and interaction. Children need it even more.

In practice, this means de-isolating the novice writer. One possibility, suggested by real-world collaborators like Nordhoff and Hall (*Mutiny on the Bounty*) and Lee and Dannay (Ellery Queen), is for children to co-author writing projects. Few experiences increase print awareness more than the battles between collaborators over wordings, ideas, and illustrations. And fewer still lead to the kind of exhilaration that occurs when minds meet. (This is something we know about first hand, having struggled with this book and each other for three years.)

As a matter of course, students should edit each other's efforts, and they should try out early drafts on classmates, teachers, and relatives. Unashamed, they should draw inspiration from the works of previous writers. If it was okay for Shakespeare and Anouilh, it's okay for your kids.

We are convinced that this kind of human interplay fosters clear, caring, and honest writing. But there are still some nitty-gritties to acknowledge.

Writer's Block. A kid can have writer's block and still put something down on paper, but the writing will be empty. This may mean nothing more than that he really had nothing to say about the given subject. (All of us have nothing to say about lots of things.) One answer is for kids to choose their own

Sometimes kids simply do not want to share their ideas with the teacher.

topics or at least develop their own slants. A "writer's conference" can also help. It's amazing how many ideas we didn't know we had in our heads until we got talking with someone else. This can be as true for a fantasy story we're making up ourselves as it is for a newspaper feature on the local hair styling salon.

A more subtle cause of writer's block is the audience. Sometimes kids simply do not want to share their ideas with the teacher. This is not necessarily a personal put-down. Many professionals express thoughts, feelings, and fantasies through their fiction that they would never express to people as close to them as your students are to you. There's no easy solution to this problem. You can't manufacture trust or openness, and anyway, you might be the wrong audience for some of your students' writing. A few teachers go out of their way to set up assignments intended for others' eyes—the student's peers, the editors of the local newspaper, a prospective real-world publisher.

Tracking Errors. While students often do have something to say about their subjects, you might

Some call for courses in logic— the problem is not in the mind but the method.

never guess it from what ended up on the page. Novices frequently get things out of order, drop crucial ideas, fail to build transitions, and permit irrelevancies to crowd out points. Professional editors say such pieces "don't track."

Incomprehensible works make kids look dumb. While some experts call for courses in logical thinking, the problem is not in the mind but the method. Almost anyone's first draft is apt to wander into chaos here and there. There's no shame in this. The shame is in leaving bad enough alone.

If students are willing to stick with it, the following techniques can be useful in putting a work onto the track. First, try to find the main thrust by summarizing the piece in a single sentence. Next, outline the draft to get a kind of x-ray picture of the underlying structure. Reading aloud, preferably with someone else around to raise questions, can uncover mispunctuation and other tracking errors.

When it comes to editing a first draft, kids should feel free to mark all over the page—crossing out irrelevancies, filling in details, and switching passages around. Many editors accomplish this last operation by actually cutting up the paper with scissors and physically rearranging sentences or paragraphs. Others prefer to decorate the page with numbers and arrows.

Prosaism. While style is largely a matter of personal preference—some people try for the swiftness of Hemingway, others are charged by the expansiveness of Wolfe—two problems typically beset the novice: triteness and wordiness.

We are trite out of habit or sloth. It's easier to use a familiar phrase than to dream up an original one. But we pay for this laziness, first by putting the reader to sleep, second by losing precision—a cliché rarely says exactly what we want to say—and third by making our writing less personal. No one ever stated the case better than George Orwell: "If thought corrupts language, language corrupts thought. . . . Phrases like *a not unjustifiable assumption, leaves much to be desired, would serve no good purpose, a consideration which we should do well to bear in mind*, are a continuous temptation, a packet of aspirins always at one's elbow. . . . This invasion of one's mind by ready-made phrases . . .

can only be prevented if one is constantly on guard against them, and every such phrase anesthetizes a portion of one's brain."°

One help is for students to learn how to use a thesaurus. They should also make a point of sticking their tongues out at themselves whenever they find they have written "green with envy," "in conclusion," "by the sweat of his brow," "depths of despair," "a good time was had by all," and "all in all, it was a beautiful experience."

Wordiness, like triteness, is largely a matter of indolence. As Mark Twain put it, "I'd have written you a shorter letter but I didn't have the time."

Needless words can mar any kind of writing. Some of the most high-sounding laws of composition (like "use the active voice") are nothing more than variations on this theme. As a single thousandth of an inch can dull a razor blade, a single unnecessary word can ruin the rhythm and sense of a one-line slogan. On the other hand, one can imagine a 600-page novel that is not a bit wordy.

The following practices should signal you that a needless word or two may have sneaked into a sentence:

1. Using the passive voice where the active would do as well.

First draft: Even if his work is not duplicated, careful consideration is given by a good writer to the visual appearance of the final draft.

Revision: Even if his work is not duplicated, a good writer gives careful consideration to the visual appearance of the final draft.

2. Repetitions of the same key word within a sentence.

First draft: One question that is commonly asked in the classroom is the question, "How long should the paper be?"

Revision: In the classroom, a common question is, "How long should the paper be?"

3. The phrases "due to," "the fact that," and "due to the fact that."

First draft: The teacher is outraged, due to the fact that he believes that students should always think in terms of quality rather than quantity.

Revision: The teacher is outraged, believing that students should always think in terms of quality rather than quantity.

4. The phrases "is what," "are what," "there is," "there are," "this is," and "these are."

First draft: Publishing is what makes the writing effort real.

Revision: Publishing makes the writing effort real.

First draft: These are duplicating methods that college towns in particular offer at reasonably low prices.

Revision: College towns in particular offer these duplicating methods at reasonably low prices.

5. The phrase "the use of."

First draft: Thus, while it is commendable for beginning writers to avoid the use of plagiarism like the plague, they are not plagiarizing if they base a piece of writing on someone else's idea.

Revision: Thus, while it is commendable for beginning writers to avoid plagiarism like the plague, they are not plagiarizing if they base a piece of writing on someone else's idea.

6. Repulsively familiar modifiers like "nice," "basic," "very," and "virtually."

First draft: The simple act of applying a stated goal to the basic format he has chosen (a very funny essay, for example) can invigorate an amateur's writing.

Revision: The simple act of applying a stated goal to the format he has chosen (a funny essay, for example) can invigorate an amateur's writing.

7. The word "one."

First draft: But the length question is a valid one.

Revision: But the length question is valid.

8. Negative statements that would mean as much in the positive.

First draft. No writer is ignorant of the power of "voice."

Revision. Every writer knows the power of "voice."

Mechanical Breakdowns. Isolated drill in "basic skills" is the most common way to teach spelling, punctuation, and usage. But is it the best way? We don't think so. For one thing, grammar lessons do not transfer reliably to a student's actual writing. Second, such exercises typically subject kids to some of the most mindless prose ever committed to print.

Grammar lessons do not transfer reliably to a student's writing.

The real value of traditional grammar instruction probably lies in teaching important print vocabulary like "agreement," "reference," and "modification," but these terms can all be learned without drill.

A more productive approach is based on real-world activities. Students pick up many mechanical skills simply by reading authentic print works and writing within authentic print formats—short story, movie review, instruction manual, newspaper. By taking the role of copy editor, they will have a chance to practice and solidify this spontaneous learning. Like the professional editors hired by publishing houses to "clean up" the work of professional writers, your students should have ready access to a dictionary, a thesaurus, a style manual, and a grammar book.

Ugliness. The antidote for footprint-marked, unillustrated, unbound assignments is the promise of publication and circulation. We tend to look our best when we know there will be lookers. Broaden the audience for your kids' efforts, show them models—books, magazines, underground poem sheets—and they will naturally raise their aesthetic sights.

The behind-the-page composing and editing practices we've outlined may seem difficult or overly complex for school children. But employed in the context of partnership and collaboration, they certainly beat the isolation-booth approach, and their cumulative effect on kids' poems, stories, articles, reviews, letters, and books can be most powerful. Indeed, as students achieve pleasure and precision in the flow of words, they will know the joy of seeing their print works become like the newspaper in the old joke—black and white and read all over.

Sources and Resources

1. Walter Gibson's description of writing pulp novels appears in his book, *The Weird Adventures of The Shadow* (New York: Grosset and Dunlap, 1960).
2. "Liquid Paper Correction Fluid" is made by Liquid Paper Corporation, Dallas, TX 75231.

3. *How to Make Your Own Books* by Harvey Weiss (New York: Thomas Y. Crowell, 1974) covers not only specific binding techniques but also a wide range of activities, including travel journals, scrapbooks, scrolls, sketchbooks, diaries, photo albums, and comic books.

4. Among the best books on writing prose are *The Elements of Style* by William Strunk and E. B. White (New York: The Macmillan Company, 1959), *Telling Writing* by Ken Macrorie (Rochelle Park, NJ: Hayden Book Company, 1970), and *The Writing and Selling of Fiction* by Paul Reynolds (Garden City, NY: Doubleday, 1965).

5. Teachers who want to try poetry writing with young children—or with older students who think they hate it—should read Kenneth Koch's *Wishes, Lies, and Dreams* (New York: Vintage, 1971).

6. James Moffett's seminal *A Student-Centered Language Arts Curriculum, Grades K-13: A Handbook for Teachers* (Boston: Houghton Mifflin Company, 1968) integrates conventional and unconventional print assignments with all sorts of language experiences, including interviewing, improvisation, speech-making, and charades.

7. The Orwell quote comes from "Politics and the English Language" in *Shooting an Elephant and Other Essays* (New York: Harcourt Brace Jovanovich, 1945).

Photography: 6
Framing the world in slides and prints

Photography democratized picture-making. Until its invention in the early nineteenth century, only a few people could create convincing, representational images of the world. Even today, less than ten percent of the population can draw. Perhaps in the future, when the sort of drawing program discussed in Chapter 4 is taught in schools, most people will be able to pick up a pencil and show you what they mean. For now, they must rely on the camera.

Magazines, newspapers, books, advertisements, posters, and filmstrips continually demonstrate how photos can be used for learning and communication. One might expect that kids would be trained in this medium from their earliest school years. But there is a problem. Photography, unlike stage, design, and print, consumes a fair amount of money. Beyond the price of a camera, it usually costs at least twenty-five cents a picture for film and developing. Thus, a ten-photo project would run about $2.50, and then only if there are no bad shots (which is roughly equivalent to assuming that *The New York Times* will contain no bad news tomorrow).

One way to save money is for kids to use their own equipment. Many families have at least one camera, and even if the student is not allowed to bring it to school, he can still do photo activities at home, a good occasion for parental involvement. If you do decide to buy cameras, you don't need one for every class member. Kids can work in groups and pass the camera around, with scheduling staggered so some children are working in photography while the rest are working in other media.

The best overall "cheap" camera is the cartridge-loading Instamatic type, available in many models starting at about $12.00. Both the newer "Pocket Instamatics" and the older "126" size are fine for most student photography projects. Less expensive cameras, the two and three dollar variety, are generally not worth the disappointing pictures they yield. If you are not interested in slides but only in prints, the popular Polaroid camera is a possibility, although the per shot cost will be slightly higher.

Many teachers have found that a good 35mm "single lens reflex" (SLR) camera is also worth the investment. (Reflex viewing means you are seeing through the lens itself, not through an auxiliary viewfinder.) When fitted out with a macro lens, this type of camera can be used for "copy work," converting magazine and book pictures of almost any size into high-quality prints or slides. Although it is possible to perform this function with the kind of Instamatic copy stand called a Visual Maker Kit, the results are decidedly inferior to what a 35mm camera can do. The Visual Maker Kit is really just an extension of the Black Box Mentality into the active phase of media (see Chapter 2), and for the price of three, a school system can buy one infinitely better SLR with a macro lens.

If your budget does not permit you to buy cameras of any kind, there are still several ways for your kids to obtain exciting photographs for classroom use. The most basic source is the "photo library," sometimes given the more colorful label, "photo morgue." Every media-oriented classroom should

Unsuccessful person photograph (top): arbitrary background elements can become disastrous disturbances.

Successful person photograph (bottom): the same subject in a less distracting environment.

have a closet or filing cabinet full of ready-made photographs ("stock shots"), including both prints and slides.

Good sources for prints are: magazines, newspapers, brochures, books, food packages, bubble gum cards, and discards from the photo collections of friends, neighbors, and members of local photo/travel clubs. Many businesses will send you photographs showing how they do what they do. Their addresses appear in the Standard and Poor's Directory, available in public libraries. Movie distributors will sometimes give stills away to a school if you convince them they're getting free publicity. We know a teacher who obtained frame blow-ups from *Jason and the Argonauts* for his course in ancient history.

Ready-made slides are available from three inexpensive sources. First, you can salvage the good shots in a damaged filmstrip by inserting them in 35mm "ready mounts." Sold in photo-supply stores, these cost less than a penny apiece. Second, you can recycle slides from projects that you no longer wish to keep. Third, you can purchase unusual slides that you or your kids are unlikely to get any other way— an astronaut on the moon, the U.N. General Assembly. (Many photo stores sell them.) The original investment in these "pro" shots is well worth it. We have used the same picture of the White House in four different slide shows.

Label each stock shot with pertinent information (who's in the shot, where and when it was taken, where you got it), and file it by rough-and-ready categories (buildings, sports, jobs, animals). If you have a school librarian who's itching for work, let him or her devise a more sophisticated cataloguing formula, perhaps based on the Dewey Decimal System.

The point of all this is that children can do photography activities in your classroom without actually handling a camera. But the heart of this medium is still the picture-taking process. Whenever possible, students should create not only organized presentations of photos, but also the photos themselves.

Concepts

In its early years, photography was often called "painting with light." Even today, when photography uses some of the most sophisticated machinery ever designed, this simple analogy stands as a basic explanation of the medium.

Photography starts with *light*, usually reflected off the subject, but sometimes coming from behind the subject (silhouettes) or even emanating from the subject itself (as in a shot of a candle). The light is collected by the *lens* and directed into the *camera body* through a tiny opening called the *aperture.* Behind the aperture is a *shutter* which moves out of the way briefly when the picture is taken, thus allowing the light to strike the film.

Like buttered bread, film consists of two parts. The "bread" part, made of clear plastic, is called the *base* and functions to hold the "butter" part of the film, the *emulsion.* The emulsion is light-sensitive and undergoes an invisible chemical change as the picture is taken. Later, when the emulsion is treated with chemicals—*developed*—the image becomes visible: a negative image in the case of film which will be used to make paper prints, and a positive image in the case of slides. A negative image on film becomes a positive image on paper because the print is actually a picture of the negative. And a negative of a negative, if you recall your algebra, is a positive.

Even elementary students can handle the developing and printing of black and white negatives (not so slides and color prints, whose processing requires precise temperature control). But if you are unable to arrange darkroom experiences, your students can still engage in what, for us, is the crux of photography—using the camera as a "third eye."

Subject

> *The camera may record exactly, but it can set down only what its operator sees, and he may see what he wants to see—what he loves and hates and pities and is proud of.*
>
> —John Steinbeck

Every good photograph has a central subject. Most subjects fit into one of five groups: *objects, places, people, events,* and *ideas.*

Novice photographers often fail to think in these categories, carelessly mixing several competing subjects in the same picture. The classic example is Aunt Minnie standing in front of the Eiffel Tower, a shot caught hopelessly in the limbo between people (Aunt Minnie) and places (the Eiffel Tower). Such photographs aren't really *about* anything.

Successful object, place, and people photographs are not just pictures that happen to include an object, a place, or a person. Rather, by emphasizing the subject over the context, the photographer lets us see it in an unusual, stimulating, or instructive way.

More complex than object, place, and people photographs are those that record a specific happening (event photographs) and those that provoke abstract thought (idea photographs). A good event photographer can approach a war, a parade, a fire, a chess tournament, or a beauty contest and come away with a picture that actually tells a story. A poor event

Unsuccessful idea photograph (top): careless composition obscures the message.

Successful idea photograph (bottom): the idea category includes staged shots—photographic equivalents to the one-panel cartoon.

photograph, on the other hand, has no more plot than a picture postcard.

Similarly, an unsuccessful idea photograph is merely a casual snapshot of poverty or racial tension or natural beauty. In a successful idea photograph, the composition is thought out, and we end up emotionally involved in what the photograph tells.

Moment

Just as the French novelist Flaubert always sought *le mot juste*, the right word, his photographic counterpart, Cartier-Bresson, sought the decisive moment. In this sense, all photographs are event photographs. The imprisoned event may be as precise as a runner's leap over a hurdle or as leisurely as a shadow's journey across a mountain. Even a still life can contain a sense of recollection—at that time it was thus.

While all pictures present "frozen moments," a fixed, finite amount of time elapses when any photograph is actually being taken. Shutter speeds typically range from 1/15 to 1/1000 of a second, but in "time lapse" shots the exposure lasts seconds, minutes, or even hours.

Thanks to rapid-fire film advance levers, the photographer may take more than one crack at the decisive moment. He can shoot a series of shots, contact print them on a "proof sheet," and then enlarge the one that, for him, is momentous.

Point of View

The photographer is a kind of dancer, moving his camera in relation to the subject until he finds a point of view that looks right. He can move closer or further, up or down, around or through, each time changing the subject's size, background, and amount of detail.

Amateurs, unfortunately, usually don't bother to choreograph their shots. Instead of walking around the subject, they settle for the first view they happen to come upon.

To increase their chances of getting an exceptional picture, professionals shoot many vantage points on the same subject. This approach, of course, assumes a large software budget. Because students do not have film to waste, they should take care to discover the "right" point of view before shooting.

Light

The photographer deals with three aspects of light: quality, quantity, and angle.

The *quality* of light is especially relevant to color photography. Sunlight is much "whiter" than the yellow of a household bulb, and film chemically "balanced" for daylight will look too yellow indoors. Similarly, indoor film looks overly blue when ex-

Contact sheet accompanied by an enlargement of the photographer's final choice.

posed outdoors. Daylight film fares better indoors under the basically green hue of a fluorescent lamp or the "blue flash" of most home photography bulbs, cubes, and strobes.

A proper *quantity* of light is needed to prevent over-exposure (image too bright) and under-exposure (image too dark). The light that actually strikes the film can be regulated by adjusting the iris diaphragm that many cameras have in front of their shutters. The photographer may use a light meter to determine the amount of light falling on or reflected from the subject, and how much to close or open the iris (what "f-stop" to use) once he has selected an optimum shutter speed.

As for a light's *angle*, the classic rule is to have most of the illumination come from behind the camera and strike the subject head-on. This reveals crucial details while preventing glare (overall washed-out quality), flare (distracting streaks), and unintentional silhouettes. With experience, professionals learn how to break this rule for effect, shooting toward the sun outdoors and, indoors, aiming lights from many different angles to soften shadows, accentuate contours, and "mold" the subject with light.

Depth

While most photographic subjects exist in three-dimensional space, photographers are not necessarily anxious to have all parts of that space in sharp focus. For any given shot, the choice of distance, exposure, and lens (wide-angle, telephoto, or normal) combine to determine the "depth of field," the thickness of space in which objects in front of and behind the main subject will also be in focus.

You can experiment with this concept by holding your thumb about a foot in front of your eye and positioning yourself about ten feet from another object. Stare at your thumb and notice how the background object becomes fuzzy. Shift your attention to the background object and your thumb will go "out of focus."

The focus control on the lens of his camera enables the photographer to select which object in a scene will be sharpest in relation to the others. If his camera has an adjustable iris and a shutter-speed control, he can actually narrow the depth of field to blur unnecessary background details and emphasize the subject, or widen the depth of field to establish the setting or include a second subject in the shot.

Context

A photograph which seems weak and unvisionary in one context can spring to life in another. Seven important ways of transforming photographs are:

This narrow-focus shot (top) was taken with a normal (50mm) lens. By moving in close, using a fast shutter speed, opening up the lens iris, and focusing on the woman with the doll, the photographer was able to make her subject stand out from its background.

This deep-focus shot (bottom) was also taken with a normal lens. You can achieve a great sense of depth by stepping back from your subject, selecting a slow shutter speed, and "stopping down" your lens as much as possible. Using a tripod helps to avoid camera jiggle when shooting at less than 1/50 of a second.

Transforming Photographs

Cropping

Combining

Designing

WOW! THEY MAKE THESE IMPORT CARS SMALLER EVERY YEAR!

Captioning

The concept of context: "finished" photographs can be endlessly manipulated for a variety of effects.

Enlarging. Almost any contact sheet will contain a few shots that you at first pass over as too complicated, yet when blown up to 8″ x 10″ or larger they become completely readable.

Cropping. When printing a photograph, it is possible to contract its borders until you find a stronger image within the original negative. A finished print can be cropped with a pair of scissors, and a slide can be cropped with opaque tape.

Cutting. Sometimes a photograph is a total loss but for a single striking element—a face, a person, a sign, an object. Here, the entire figure should be cut out along its contours for use in a new context (a locket, a mobile, a Christmas tree ornament).

Combining. A small photo can be pasted on top of a larger one to synthesize new objects, people, scenes, or events.

Designing. Photographs are often included in a larger design context, as in collages, record jackets, magazine articles, and advertisements.

Sequencing. The meaning and impact of a photograph can change completely when it is included in a sequence of several photographs.

Captioning. Supplementary words, like supplementary pictures, can give a photograph new meaning. Captions needn't always run along the bottom of the photograph. Many photo-posters include a caption as part of their design, and dialogue balloons can be pasted directly onto a picture for humorous or narrative effects.

Activities

Because the photograph has two distinct forms—slides and prints—most of the following ideas adapt to both large group showings and individual "readings." The virtue of slide shows is that they can be accompanied by prerecorded music, voices, or natural sounds. Printed photographs, on the other hand, have the advantage of instant availability. They don't require a projector, an extension cord, a screen and a darkened room.

The Photo Portrait

The biographer creates a word-picture of another human being. The photographer, too, can provide insights into a person's life. Just as a good biography goes beyond surface facts, a good photo portrait goes beyond surface appearances. The subject's spirit, accomplishments, and milieu all matter.

Instamatics are poorly adapted to close-up work, so if your kids are using this type of camera they will not be able to take conventional full-face portraits. This seeming drawback can become a virtue, forcing the photographer to step back and consider his subject's environment. A dull wall or an arbitrary door won't do; the photographer must place the person in a context which informs. A gregarious individual might be portrayed with friends around, a loner by himself on a park bench. Action also enhances photo portraits. What activities characterize the subject? Show her with her trumpet, her catcher's mitt, her dog, her typewriter.

In an English or foreign language context, this format can be coupled with essay writing: My Father, My Pen Pal, My Gang. In a unit on psychology, kids can use photo portraits to learn what people reveal—and hide—when they know they're being captured on film. A good social studies/geography project for kicking off the school year has each student shooting a photo portrait of another class member, pasting it alongside a map of the neighborhood, and drawing a line to the location of his subject's house.

The Photo Illustration

Photography has long rivaled drawing as a way to illustrate books, newspapers, magazines, advertisements, packages, and lectures. Sometimes, of course, the abstracting and fantasy-making powers of design make it the better medium for getting a message across. Whenever students face the problem of visualizing events, processes, and concepts in the course of their school work, they must first decide whether to use photos or drawings or both.

Kids can use photo illustrations as the "visual half" of their articles, reviews, stories, poems, booklets, and other print projects. An important issue is layout—integrating the photograph with the text instead of plopping it down any old place. For real-world models of good photo spreads, students can analyze articles and ads in magazines like *Newsweek, Scientific American, Sports Illustrated*, and *Psychology Today.*

The Photo Essay

In a photo essay the pictures do not simply illustrate a print project—they are the project's primary means of communication. What prose there is follows up the visuals, clarifying, filling in, or making transitions.

Some photo essays consist of only a few shots. Others have hundreds. The photos should be assembled as a book or mounted on a large sheet of cardboard. They should be arranged sequentially, not as a collage, and captioned if necessary. The essential problem is to offer the viewer a "study" of a particular object, place, person, event, or process. Children do best starting close to home. One popular format is *The Many Faces of* . . . my town, my pet, my mother's job, my school.

There are two rules for writing the captions. First, be brief. Second, complement the picture with provocative information, as opposed to telling the self-evident. Don't write: "Here we have me reading one of my favorite comic books." Write: "At the end of a hard day, I like to curl up with some good literature."

A particularly striking kind of photo essay shows change over time. It is a compelling paradox that photographs "freeze" time and yet are able, when properly sequenced, to communicate a sense of processes unfolding. This effect is especially dramatic when the camera offers the same point of view for each shot in the essay.

Given the significance of process and change in almost every branch of knowledge, one can hardly overstate the utility of photo-sequencing. In science, for example, it can be used to learn about the growth of molds, plants, or crystals; the construction of buildings; the progress of the seasons; the physical development of people.

Many photo essays work equally well as slide essays. Instead of captions, the producer provides verbal commentary (assuming any is needed). Slides also lend themselves to full-fledged soundtracks, which brings us to the next activity.

The Slide-Tape

Like the genius who first combined peanut butter with jelly, the inventor of the slide-tape is nameless. But we should all take our lens caps off to him or her. Few media formats make the processes of selecting, timing, and arranging images so purposeful and concrete.

A slide-tape is a sequence of slides accompanied by a prerecorded, synchronized tape featuring any or all of the basic sounds: music, narration, dialogue, noises. A good slide-tape soundtrack is very much like a good radio play or sound essay. (See Chapter 7.)

Any issue handled by instructional films or commercially prepared filmstrips can be developed into a slide-tape. In fact, sound filmstrips are nothing more than efficiently (inflexibly) packaged slide-tapes. We've seen outstanding junior and senior high student programs on such subjects as the life of Martin Luther King, Jr., religious communes in Massachusetts, and the Ivory Coast in Africa.

Most slide-tape projects begin with the student selecting a topic and then collecting an appropriate set of slides. Next he writes a script connecting his knowledge of the topic to the particular images at his disposal. The script is usually done second be-

Any issue handled by instructional films or filmstrips can be developed into a slide-tape.

cause it's easier to find words to go with slides than vice versa.

The biggest mistake one can make when scripting a slide-tape is telling the audience what they can see for themselves: "This slide shows you the Hancock Building's many broken windows." Instead, the commentary should stand as an essay in itself: "The planners of Boston's Hancock Building forgot to account for high-altitude wind velocities when specifying window glass strength." An audience's involvement with a slide-tape is almost always greater when they must connect the sounds to the images.

Occasionally it's best to work on script, photography, and soundtrack in alternation—shooting the initial slides, for example, then conducting an interview, then taking additional slides that now seem called for, then rewriting a part of the narration. Sometimes the student will begin with a completed soundtrack (essay, interview, symphony, poem, song) and then set about obtaining the visuals it suggests.

It's surprising how effective a slide-tape interpretation of a poem or song can be. In theory, the slides should seem redundant because a song has its own imagery. In practice, audiences are fascinated to see what pictures the photographer settled on to illustrate even the most familiar works. The changing of the slides in correspondence with the lyrics can amplify a song's meaning or underscore its structure. Slides can also be used in "counterpoint" with a song, reversing or lampooning its intention. In one memorable slide-tape, shown on a now-defunct TV program, shots documenting the drearier realities of urban life accompanied the pop hit, "Downtown." ("Things'll be great when you're downtown. . . .")

Slide-tapes can tell fictional stories, a format we call "the living comic book." The first step is to break the story into significant moments. Each shot should move the plot along, but not leap so far ahead that the viewer is confused. The acting must be bold and large; subtle gestures usually won't register. Costumes and props—a wild mask, a knife sticking out of an actor's back—help the story come alive. The living comic can dramatize historical events, biographies, or serious literature. Like regular comics, the form also lends itself to humor.

The first question teachers ask us about slide-tape production is "How do you synchronize the slides with the soundtrack?" The answer is, quite simply, "by hand." Numerous devices now on the market, including "slide-synch" cassette tape recorders and "carousel programmers," enable you to put "synch signals" on a tape. Upon replay, the signals automatically advance each slide at the appropriate point in the show. These machines are nice, but not essential.

They won't do anything memory can't, and even the best of them start acting finicky before long. We would even argue that it's character-building for students to run their slide-tapes manually, thinking on their feet and anticipating each cue.

The other common question is "How long should each image stay on the screen?" There are no rules about this, other than horse sense. Even if you show an authentic shot of Adam and Eve before The Fall, after about fifteen seconds the audience will be calling for the next slide. The program's aural content—narration, song, interview, whatever—should dictate how many slides to use and when to advance each.

The Photo Exhibit

Although the preceding activities invite artistry, they are all examples of applied photography. Professional photographers would term them assignments.

But there is another, "purer" sort of picture-taking in which the photographer goes out with his camera for the sole purpose of discovering images that please. When your students produce such shots, encourage them to create a photo exhibit.

Unlike a photo essay, a photo exhibit does not present a fixed sequence that must be read in a particular order. The theme, if there is one, is not formally studied but informally explored. The captions, if there are any, are usually limited to titles or impressionistic remarks.

Students can publish their photo exhibits in the local newspaper or hang them in the school (front hall, library, main office) or in the community (restaurants, banks, stores). For unconventional displays, mount the photographs on something besides a wall—on the faces of a box (photo cube); on strings (photo mobile); on a poster in some kind of patterned relationship to each other (photo collage); on the inside surfaces of a box containing an electric light and a peep hole (phototorium); or even on houseplants, bottles, driftwood or styrofoam packing material. These particular mounting formats can also be used for "assignment" type shots dealing with classroom issues—a photo collage about urban sprawl, for example, or a photo cube about Edgar Allan Poe's mind.

Standards

The greatest barrier to taking good photographs is unintentionally summed up in the title of a popular student photo booklet: "It's So Simple—Click and Print." Authentic photography, as opposed to camera clicking and snapshot nabbing, is not simple. The

SLIDES	SOUNDTRACK	SLIDES	SOUNDTRACK

Hi! We're a third grade class from Byam School. We want to tell you how we became writers, editors, and publishers of our own stories.

The next day we finally began being editors. We divided up into two groups. One group worked in pairs. We looked at each partner's story and found things that needed to be corrected.

First of all, we had to decide what to write about.

The other group had conferences with the teacher. Next we carefully wrote our corrected stories over onto a final white piece of paper. Some of us added illustrations.

We could choose anything from lovely fairy tales to exciting sports adventures.

After all that thinking, it was time to get down to business. We spent a lot of time getting our ideas as perfect as possible.

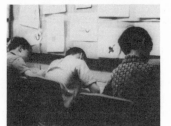

Now we were finally ready to be publishers. Some of us hung our stories on the bulletin board for everyone to read. Some of us copied our stories onto masters and ran them off in the office.

Then we bound them together into story books. This is the end of our own story of what we do as authors, illustrators, editors, and publishers. Try it sometime!

Edited exerpts from an elementary school slide-tape. Note the diversity of the images (live action shots, magazine collages, original art) and how some slides are shown without any words. The narration was written and read by the children. Their teacher operated the camera and tape recorder.

SUBJECT	
person	_____
place	_____
thing	_____
happening	_____
nothing in particular	_____
LIGHTING	
too bright	_____
too dark	_____
correct	_____
POINT OF VIEW	
too close	_____
too far	_____
correct	_____
FRAMING	
poorly-placed subject	_____
well-placed subject	_____
SHARPNESS	
blurred	_____
crisp	_____
COMMENTS	

Student photo exhibit (top) and photo review chart (bottom).

act of slicing a visual moment from life, even with an Instamatic, involves many concerns: having a good subject, finding the best perspective, making sure the light is right, shooting at the decisive moment, and, of course, avoiding such technical errors as:

Blurred Image: The slightest camera jiggle can blur a photograph. Have kids practice the photographer's stance—feet well planted, arms close to the body, camera pressed firmly against the face. Whenever possible, use a tripod, especially for shooting "laboratory" set-ups like aquariums, mold gardens, or chemical reactions.

Dark Image. Never overestimate the power of a flash cube. Instamatic strobe lights are even weaker. When using these devices, stay between four to seven feet from the subject.

Washed-Out Image. Don't shoot into a window. Don't shoot into the sun. Don't take pictures that are mostly sky. Don't use flash cubes closer than three feet.

We've also found that the chart on this page can help kids become more critical of their photographs. The idea is to move them beyond global reactions— "This one stinks"—to the kind of evaluation a professional might do.

When introducing the chart to kids, start with photographs taken by strangers. (For large groups, use slides.) This way students can slam the shots without damaging anyone's ego. The greatest learning comes when the class graduates from saying what's technically wrong with a photograph to saying how it might have been made more effective in terms of the six concepts: subject, moment, point of view, light, depth, and context. ("If only the photographer had waited until the diver left the board," "If only the background weren't so busy," "If only she had stepped back far enough to get the snake's rattle into the frame.")

If you've ever had the experience of watching a "home slide show" in which each image evokes a ten-minute non-story from the projectionist, you know another common pitfall of amateur photography. The idea that a picture is worth a thousand words doesn't mean that anybody wants to hear a thousand words about it. Rather, the photograph should be allowed to stir up a swarm of thoughts and feelings inside the viewer's head.

This is really the major criterion that classroom photo productions should be measured against. Do the pictures say something beyond the words with which they are juxtaposed? Do they stand as statements on their own? Do they tell us what the photographer "loves and hates and pities and is proud of"?

1. Teachers seeking a strong handle on basic photography can do no better than the first three volumes of the famous *Time-Life Library of Photography*, available in many camera stores and from Time-Life Books in New York.

2. A complete-it-yourself photography manual for elementary school children is Murray Suid's *Painting with the Sun*, available from Dynamic Learning Corporation, 60 Commercial Wharf, Boston, MA 02110. The book includes projects that very young children can do successfully.

3. A lively little publication for the slightly-advanced photographer is *The Nikon School of Photography Handbook*. Write to Ehrenreich Photo-Optical Industries, 623 Stewart Avenue, Garden City, NY 11530.

Radio: 7
Seeing with the ear

The seven-hundred foot mountain of whipped cream started rolling toward Lake Michigan, which had been drained for the occasion and filled with hot chocolate. *Splash!* Next, the Canadian Royal Air Force appeared overhead, towing a ten-ton maraschino cherry. At a prearranged signal, the bombardier released the cherry—*Plop!*—into the whipped cream, while 25,000 bystanders cheered their approval. And radio was right there, bringing the entire event into our living rooms.

Stan Freberg, a comedian who understands radio the way a bat understands radar, devised his famous "giant sundae" routine in the early Sixties as a response to the emerging medium of television.° He was tired of hearing the aphorism that "radio is nothing more than blind television." In Freberg's view, every medium creates a complete experience for us. Just as looking at a photograph or a painting doesn't make us feel deaf, hearing a radio drama or sound essay or interview show doesn't make us feel blind. Instead, we see with our inner eye of imagination. There are times when such imagery clearly outclasses that of TV and film.

Of course, the imagination-stirring power of radio would mean little to you as a teacher if tapping it required a 50,000-watt transmitter and an FCC license. Fortunately, you need neither. Every radio format—drama, news, commercials, music, two-way talk radio, sound essays—can be convincingly simulated on quarter-inch or cassette audiotape. What you're really after is disembodied sound. The essence of radio is performing without being seen.

You could get something of this effect by having your students act behind a screen. But then they would not be able to learn by hearing themselves. In addition, they would give up much of the technical control, like editing, that tape makes possible.

And why give up something that costs so little? Audio recording is probably the cheapest of modern media. Almost every school has some sort of tape recorder kicking around, and that old workhorse reel-to-reel machine gathering dust in the bottom of the A-V closet will serve you as well as a brand-new cassette portable. An hour's worth of tape costs less than $3.00 and is reusable.

None of this means that student radio productions cannot find a mass outlet. Without the fuss of an assembly, they may be shared throughout the school by passing the tape recorder from classroom to classroom or by playing tapes over the school intercom. Since many families have tape recorders, a student's sound work can also be heard at home by his parents.

More spectacularly, classroom radio can reach the public at large. Try sending outstanding tapes to your local radio station with the helpful hint that they be played in partial fulfillment of the FCC requirement for public-service broadcasting. College radio stations in particular are often eager to air amateur productions.

Concepts

Sound productions can be incredibly simple ("Hello, this is Murray Suid talking, but I'm not really here. When you hear the beep give your name and number. . . .") or devilishly complex (Freberg's giant sundae bit combined voice effects, sound effects, and narration into a perfectly orchestrated drama). In either case, the same five production concepts must be considered.

Program

One of the authors recalls his parents' purchase of a tape recorder some two decades ago. There was great excitement as the adults threaded up the magical device, recorded a few seconds, and then played back the immortal "1 . . 2 . . . 3 . . . testing . . . testing. Is it on? What should I say? Let's hear it . . . ."

Talk about Narcissus! We spent the whole evening enraptured by our voices saying nothing, the vacuum cleaner buzzing, the phone ringing, Uncle Abe snoring. But the machine soon lost its novelty because after you found out it could mirror things, so what?

It wasn't until a few weeks later when an older kid visited us that we really got into the thing. He knew how to make neat sound effects—drumming his fingers on the table to simulate galloping horses—and he showed us the hair-raising power of screams. Within an hour, we put together a horror-cowboy drama complete with a commercial: "Lost . . . L . . . O . . . S . . . T . . . Lost. Tell your little brother to go down to the corner and get Lost." If *you* don't want to get lost—with radio—first develop a program concept.

Sounds

Every radio production includes one or more of the following sound images: 1) voice, 2) music, 3) natural sounds (often called "sound effects"), 4) ambience, and 5) silence. Each makes a special appeal to the imagination. Take voice for example. Most of us have had the experience of talking on the telephone to someone we've never seen. Often we are taken aback when we actually meet the person because his or her physical appearance fails to conform to the mental picture we formed on the phone.

Ambience refers to the sense of physical space a recording communicates. A tape made in a large hallway does not "feel" the same as one made in a tiny studio. The distinction results from that multitude of audio images that are usually too subtle to be consciously noticed—the rush of air, minor echoes, distant traffic or air conditioner rumblings. Sound artists assume that ambient noise is separate from articulated sound effects like bells clanging and doors slamming and needs to be controlled as an entity in itself.

Silence is a two-fold issue. On the one hand, there's unintentional silence: "We now bring you the stock report featuring Warren Wintergreen at the New York Stock Exchange. Take it away Warren. . . . . Warren? Are you there? . . . . ." This kind of silence, sometimes called "dead air time," is anathema to radio people because, if it continues for long, listeners may conclude that the station has gone off the air.

But there is another kind of silence: intended pauses that heighten tension, build rhythm, or surprise. It takes daring to use this negative space as a radio image, just as it does to use broad areas of white canvas in painting. Purposeful silence is often indicated in scripts by ellipses (. . .).

Miking

The microphone ("mike") in a sound production is analogous to the camera in a film or television show. Its relationship to its subject is not necessarily detached or static. The mike can express something in itself.

Most radio is done "on mike." The performers position themselves close to the microphone and speak directly into it. But sometimes it is more appropriate, or at least more practical, to record someone slightly "off mike" (the interviewer in an interview tape, for example) or at a great distance from the mike (say, to communicate an overall impression of a factory, so ambience and machine noises become as important as talk). In radio drama, it often makes sense for actors to move to one side of the microphone while speaking. This kind of "dynamic miking" can reinforce any number of impressions suggested by the dialogue: that a character is searching for something under a table, that someone is crossing the room, that the scene is ending.

Radio directors strive to make their mikes "invisible." They want listeners to forget about the microphone *per se* and become involved in the show. In conventional radio production, the microphone is not held by the performers but fixed to a stand. This minimizes the chances of an actor absentmindedly fiddling with the cord or tapping the mike's casing. Mike noise is every bit as jarring and distracting to a radio audience as camera jiggling is to a movie audience.

Editing

As fans of courtroom drama know, tape recordings are suspect evidence because they are so susceptible to editing. Portions can be left out, sections rearranged, new material inserted. For the amateur, editing can prove tricky because tape, unlike movie film, doesn't allow you to literally see where you are. You have to *hear* where you are by replaying the recording and stopping it precisely where you want to edit it.

Editing can be done *physically* by cutting and splicing the tape. A good tape splicer will come with instructions, and the inside of a tape box sometimes contains splicing tips. Editing can be done *electronically* by selectively transferring segments of a tape being played on a "master" machine to a tape being recorded on a "slave" machine. The audio signal is carried on a "patch cord" connecting the recorders. Electronic splices are usually called "edits."

Once you master the technique, you may prefer electronic editing to physical editing. For one thing, you can redo an edit easily if you find you unintentionally clipped a syllable or extended a pause. (With physical splicing, a crucial bit of sound you didn't realize you were omitting can get lost forever.) Also, since your original reels remain intact you can save them for reemployment in future shows or, conversely, recycle them as "splice-free" tape—almost as good as new. A third advantage of electronic editing is that your master tapes can be recorded in both directions. Physical splices in a two-track tape cut into the second track (commonly called "second side") and alter its content as well.

While editing brings to mind spy-like intrigues, it can also make amateur productions infinitely more polished. We know a Philadelphia teacher who used to edit the "uhs" out of kids' taped speeches to show them how they could sound with practice. (This kind of precision is possible only with open-reel tape and is one of many advantages this format holds over the cassette format.)

Mixing

Audio buffs talk about the "transparency" of sound. When sound images are mixed together, they do not cancel each other out. Static, tape hiss, surface noise, and amplifier hum will come through a radio's speaker just as readily as music or voices. But transparency also presents artistic advantages. Music can be mixed "under" dialogue to reinforce the mood of a drama. Noises and ambience recorded at different times can be blended into a totally new environment.

In one sense, every microphone is also a "mixer" since it will record whatever simultaneous sounds come within its range. The relative volume of each image is often a simple function of the distance between the microphone and the sound source. Thus, the easiest way for an amateur to do a mix is to play

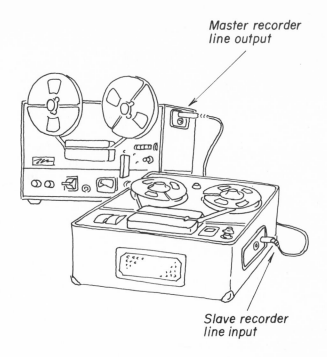

Master recorder line output

Slave recorder line input

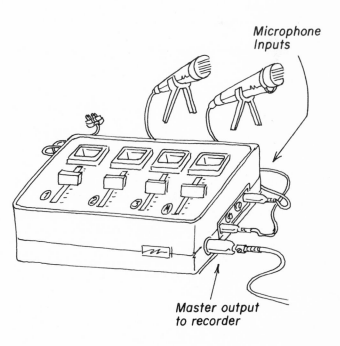

Microphone Inputs

Master output to recorder

An electronic editing set-up (top) and a microphone mixer (bottom).

secondary sounds (from records and tapes) in the background.

Professionals want more control over mixing. The box-shaped device called a "mixer" enables a radio technician to connect several microphones, each with its own volume control, to a single tape recorder. In the Thirties and Forties, radio production was usually done by mixing at least three mikes—typically, two for the actors and one for the sound effects. The next breakthrough was multichannel (stereophonic, quadrophonic, etc.) tape recording. Now sound artists could create a basic recording or "track," rewind the tape, and record a second track while listening to the first. Modern recording studios can "lay down" as many as thirty-two simultaneous tracks.

Activities

A science fiction story called "Voices" describes the efforts of earth scientists to pick up alien radio broadcasts and thereby discover the nature of extraterrestrial intelligence. At a crucial point, one of the characters wonders if beings on other worlds are "out there" listening to earth. For over fifty years, a smorgasbord of news, comedy, music, preaching, pitching, politicking, and more has leaped from the face of the earth to who-knows-where? What would aliens make of us if they judged us by our commercial radio broadcasts?

The character who posed this question shuddered. But if aliens have a sense of humor and a bit of objectivity, they might be delighted or even awestruck. There's been junk on junk, who can deny it? But also an incredible amount of creative production.

Seven particular radio production activities follow. In each case, we suggest that you play an example of the format before the students try using it themselves. (Sources for appropriate tapes and discs appear at the end of the chapter.)

The Candid Microphone Show

Because it requires minimal scripting, "candid microphone" makes a good introductory radio activity. The major part of the producer's ingenuity is consumed in hiding the mike and devising situations which get the "victims" to perform.

One important caution: Allen Funt, father of "Candid Microphone" and "Candid Camera," was careful not to embarrass people or invade their privacy. Etiquette requires that your kids inform the subject that he or she has been recorded. If the response is "Okay, you got me," feel free to use the tape. If the person is upset, erase it immediately. (The curricular uses of candor are more extensive

than you might suppose—see the discussion of "The Candid Camera Show" in Chapter 9.)

The Disc-jockey Show

There are as many styles of disc-jockeying as there are styles of music. Bring an AM-FM radio to class and station-hop with your kids for an unforgettable lesson in voice variability: loud and soft, fast and slow, raspy and smooth, serious and ironic. Note how formats vary. Some DJ's explain the music, others tell jokes.

To produce their own DJ shows, students will need a record player, a stack of records, and a tape recorder. Once they get the patter down, kids can DJ their way into all kinds of learning. Even an abstruse subject like economics can get the treatment via songs like "If I Were a Rich Man" or "The Best Things in Life Are Free" interspersed with stock market reports, world trade news, and ads for the Common Market.

Professional disc-jockey shows inevitably include commercials. In context, most of them come across as annoying distractions. A few, however, are worth taping off the air and analyzing for their ingenious mixture of art and hustle.

Some students may prefer to prerecord their radio commercials and play them back during the show, as real-world DJ's do. (This, of course, requires a second tape recorder.) Partly for the sake of authenticity, but more for an experience in discipline, have kids limit their commercials to 15, 30, or 60 seconds. No other assignment better demonstrates what brevity has to do with wit and the importance of word choice in communicating. The time constraint gives students a chance to polish their performances. When your bit lasts 15 seconds, it's easy to rehearse it ten, twenty, or a hundred times.

Commercials need not be limited to services and products. Students can produce *Sesame Street*-type "spots" for vocabulary words, number facts, books (instead of book reports), and science laws. They can even create historical commercials—for example, a one-minute recruitment ad George Washington might have pitched from Valley Forge.

The Radio Play

Three thousand years before the advent of "blind TV," another blind medium, Homer, kept audiences spellbound with his dramatic renditions of the *Iliad* and the *Odyssey*. And surely the oral tradition was ancient before Homer opened his mouth.

Given this venerable history, the continuing interest in radio drama and comedy is no surprise. Part of it, to be sure, is attributable to nostalgia, fond memories of The Shadow or Fibber McGee and

Molly. But nostalgia doesn't explain phenomena like the National Public Radio Theater or the CBS Radio Mystery Theater, which as of this writing air original radio plays to stations throughout the country. Apparently the oral-aural magic still works —and it can work for your kids. With a decent tape recorder, a record player, and a tableful of handmade sound effect devices, students can spin out sweeping panoramas, space trips, enchanted glens, historic battles, robots, talking animals, all within a ten by ten cubicle.

The methods are not intuitive. Making radio shows isn't like talking on the telephone; bringing a play to life involves such sophisticated conventions as dialogue, narration, sound effects, and transitions. The best way to teach these conventions is to point them out as the class listens to an authentic radio recording.

Dialogue is what the characters in a radio play say. One important trick of writing radio dialogue is "tagging"—indicating within a line the person spoken to. "What do you want from me, Phillip?" (Phillip is the tag, and he will probably have the next line.) "I think you *know* what I want, Mason." (Now it's clear that the previous line was Mason's.) Without tags, radio conversation gets jumbled and difficult to follow.

Narration includes the opening and closing patter of the show's host or announcer, as well as the verbal storytelling of an omniscient observer (often the host, but sometimes an unidentified speaker). The storytelling dimension of radio narration is notable for its frequent use of the "second person" (also a common comic book device). This technique almost never works in print, but in radio our host is always telling us things like "Well, Nancy Stapleford, there's no turning back now—you've arranged the perfect crime and your only other choice is a long stretch in prison for attempted murder."

Radio dialogue and narration provide great opportunities for "voice play." Have kids listen to, and try to imitate, the voices of senior citizens, babies, famous personalities, and people in special vocations such as telephone operator, sportscaster, eyewitness reporter, public address announcer, telephone time-voice, dial-a-prayer minister, or police dispatcher. For pure fantasy, there is always the talking pencil, the talking Venus flytrap, and the Martian who's lost in Ashtabula. Suggest tricks like speaking with the nose pinched or talking into cloth, mailing tubes, and buckets.

Sound effects can increase our involvement in a show by forcing us to interpret what we are hearing. Instead of an undramatic bit of narration like "The blackmailer called Sally's worried parents on the

```
PHIL MORGAN-I

MUSIC:   Theme up & under:
ANNR.:   Phil Morgan, Private Detective!
MUSIC:   Theme UP & out.
MORGAN   (Narr.):  My name is Phil Morgan.  Private detective.  This
                   was one of my earliest cases.  It took place 8
                   years ago, as you'll see by looking in my files.
                   Now, here is the case of THE NEW WEAPON.
DUN:     Well, Breen, I'll be seein' ya.  I've got just enough time
         to pick up Shirley and take her to the restaurant.
BREEN:   OK, Dun, I'll lock up.
DUN (Fading):  OK.  'Bye, Breen.
SOUND:   DOOR CLOSES OFF.
BREEN (Self):  Well, I guess I--(KNOCK ON DOOR OFF)  Yeah, who's
         there?
SOUND:   DOOR OPENS OFF:  GUN SEQUENCE.
MUSIC:   Bridge.
MORGAN   (Narr.):  I had an appointment to see Bob Breen, an old
                   friend of mine, at his store in New Crudbug.
SOUND:   CAR HALTS:  OUT OF CAR:  DOOR CLOSES:  STEPS:  KNOCK ON DOOR.
MORGAN:  Hey, Breen!  (KNOCK)  Bob, open up!  It's me, Morgan!  (KNOCK)
         Hey!  (Self)  That's strange.  He said he'd be here.  Maybe
         someone murdered him.  (Narr.)  So I tried the door.  It
         was unlocked, so I just walked in.
SOUND:   DOOR OPEN, CLOSE.
MORGAN:  Hey, Bob!  Bob!  --Wha--!  (RUNNING STEPS)  Bob!  Shot in the
         back, head, leg, thigh, stomach, arm, ear, and ankle!
         Bob!  Are you hurt?!
MUSIC:   Sting.
MORGAN   (Narr.):  I called for an ambulance.  It took a little while
                   to arrive.
SOUND:   AMBULANCE ARRIVES.
MORGAN:  Well, doc?
DOCTOR:  It's too late.  He's dead.
MORGAN:  Thank goodness it's not anything serious!
MUSIC:   Sympathy.
MORGAN   (Narr.):  I used to know Bob when I was in the Army during
                   the war.  I shot him accidentally, thinking he was
                   my CO.  After that, we became good friends.  Both
                   of us got the CO.  Now the problem was:  who murdered
                   him?  But I didn't know much else about him, except
                   that he had a wife.
MORGAN:  Mrs. Breen, I'm Phil Morgan.  I'm investigating your hus-
         band's death.
MRS. BREEN:  Oh, yeah?
MORGAN:  Were you and your husband happily married?
MRS. BREEN:  Why, ya think I killed him or somethin'?
MORGAN:  I have to know, Mrs. Breen.
MRS. BREEN:  Bob was a lout.  He ate like a horse and made the house
         look like a pig-pen.  And he treated me like a slave.
         We hated each other and got into fights every night.
         Sure, we were happily married.
MUSIC:   Bridge.
MORGAN:  Well, thank you, Mrs. Breen.  I guess I'll be going.
MRS. BREEN:  Say, gumshoe.  Try findin' Maxie Mushmouth.  He useta
         work for Bob.  Hated him.
MORGAN:  Thanks.  (Narr.):  So that was a blank, except for this Max-
         ie Mushmouth.  I went back to my car.
```

Radio play script-excerpt by Ron Harris, age 14. Note that some sound effect cues are mixed in with the dialogue, a trick that helps the engineer to produce each noise at precisely the right moment.

phone," there might be the sound of a phone being dialed and then the blackmailer saying, "Hello, Mr. Jenkins, I have your daughter."

There are two ways to get sound effects into a production. The first is sound effects discs. By scrounging in record shops, you can unearth every conceivable audio image from an atom bomb blast to a chicken laying an egg. The trouble with discs is that they must be cued up (or "spotted" as some radio directors say) on a record player so the sound will be heard at the right moment. This can be tricky with nonprofessional equipment run by nonprofessionals. (One partial solution is to prerecord particular selections on a separate tape in the desired order and play this tape on a second machine.)

The other approach is to manufacture sounds "live" during the production. This requires a sound effects "artist" who stands ready at a table filled with the following sorts of materials: a doorbell, an old phone, a pan of water, a pan of gravel (for walking on), a loud ticking clock (time bomb). A few classic effects can be produced as shown on this page.

Kids can also use their own voices to make sirens, wind, airplane engines, and explosions. While sound effects should be subordinate to the drama, kids will have fun producing them and may even get a script idea from an intriguing squeak or boink.

One important aspect of scripting radio sound effects is called "planting." Because we get more cues from our eyesight than we realize, noises heard in isolation are sometimes hard to identify. Radio scripts often have the characters comment on sounds:

(**Sound:** Footsteps and cell door squeaking)

Lamont: They're coming, Dan!

The "they're coming" serves to "plant" the footfalls and squeaking and thus helps us to correctly identify these images. Planting is to sound effects what tagging is to dialogue.

In every narrative form, *transitions* between scenes are a major concern. Filmmakers rely on fade-outs and dissolves. Novelists use chapter divisions. Theater directors can bring down the curtain or dim the lights. In radio, the transitions are more subtle, but they are no less crucial.

The simplest way to indicate the end of a scene in a radio play is for the actor, while saying the last line, to move into the mike's "dead area"—the space to the side where most microphones do not pick up sound well—so that his voice fades out. The same result can be achieved by turning down the "record volume" as the show is being taped.

Fire. Crinkle cellophane six inches from the microphone.

Bird flying. Shake a partly opened umbrella up and down.

Breaking down a door. Crunch a piece of balsa wood in a fist held near the mike.

Rain. Trickle grains of rice onto a sheet of paper stretched tightly above the mike.

Telephone voice. Place the mike near the receiver and have the actor call the studio.

Chase through underbrush. Beat two leafy twigs together.

Guillotine. Chop a head of cabbage on a cutting board placed near the mike.

The other basic transition device is the "music bridge." In a typical bridge, music starts immediately at the end of a scene, continues for a few seconds, then fades "under and out" as the opening dialogue or narration of the next scene comes in "over" it. This effect is usually indicated by the directions "music in full and under" and "music out."

Sometimes a "cross-fade" gets us from one scene to the next. In this technique, analogous to a dissolve in a movie, the closing music, sound effect, or voice of a scene is "faded out" while the opening music, sound effect, or voice of the next scene is simultaneously "faded up."

Years ago, radio plays were published on a regular basis. Although some of these volumes can still be unearthed in library basements and used-book stores, your students will probably prefer to write their own scripts, inspired by favorite stories, TV shows, or heroes and heroines of their own making. One good source of adaptable material is comic books. Comics supply dialogue (in the balloons), sound effects, and often narration.

Once the student feels comfortable with radio play conventions, he can apply this activity to his studies. Via the tried and tested "You Are There" format, for example, he can portray historical events—everything from the sailing of the Mayflower to the discovery of penicillin. Such projects transform the chore of library research into a kind of treasure hunt for authentic, dramatizable material.

Of course, a script is nothing until captured on tape. Because radio performers always have their scripts in front of them, there is a special danger of the dialogue sounding like it's being read rather than spoken. To avoid stumbling, student radio actors should practically memorize their lines. At the same time, they should strive for a delivery which makes it seem that the characters are saying their words for the first time. The end product of rehearsal should be naturalness, not glibness.

Rehearsal is also crucial for getting cues and timing right, especially if many sound effects are required. With extremely complex scripts, students will occasionally have to stop the tape in the middle of a production to catch their breath, prepare the next scene, or correct a spectacular line fluff. But be careful they do not become overly dependent on the erasing capability. The best radio productions are done as sustained performances, not in bits and pieces.

The Newscast

The challenge of newscasting is voice modulation. Tragic stories require sober tones. Human interest

The best radio productions are done as sustained performances, not in bits and pieces.

"How Do You Feel About Racial Violence?"

Interview 1

SAM: I'm doing an interview. I'd like to know what you think about racial violence.

WOMAN: Racial violence? (pause) I don't approve of it. I think we can all live in peace if we really tried.

SAM: Well, how do you think, uh, we could do anything on stopping racial violence?

WOMAN: Hmm. On stopping it? Stopping it? I don't know.

SAM: Okay. Thank you.

Interview 2

SAM: Do you have a minute for, I'm doing...

WOMAN: I don't have a minute for nothing.

SAM: Okay.

Interview 3

SAM: I'm conducting an interview for Shaw Junior High and I'd like to ask you a question. What do you think about racial violence?

MAN: I think it's bad.

SAM: Do you approve of police brutality to stop racial violence?

MAN: NO, no.

SAM: Do you have any speical reasons for not approving?

MAN: Well, I think they ought to treat a case as they find it.

Interview 4

SAM: I'm conducting an interview for Shaw Junior High School, and I'd like to ask you, do you approve of racial violence?

WOMAN: Do I approve of racial violence?!! I should say not!

SAM: Well, uh...

WOMAN: I think you boys are going to get further if you cut that out.

SAM: Yes. Do you think they should use police brutality when they're having racial violence?

WOMAN: Well, I think they should use it down there at the administration building because my aerial was broke on my car. And I thought they were going to break my windshield and drag me out of the car. Now, people who are criticizing didn't see that. (lowers her voice) Look, look, I'm for the colored every time, but when this violence comes...what would they have done to me if they pulled me out of that car?

SAM: Yes.

WOMAN: I'm a teacher and I know. So, I hope you boys get on top, but please get together and get rid of this (voice trembles) violence.

Interview 5

SAM: I'm doing interviews for Shaw and I'd like to ask you what do you, uh, how do you feel about racial violence?

POLICEMAN: I think it's stupid, to tell you the truth.

SAM: Okay. Well, how do you think we should, what do you, what method do you think we should use to stop racial violence when it, uh, when it occurs.

POLICEMAN: What method? (pause) Stop it, I'd stop it as it begins, I would. Don't let it get out of hand. Otherwise, innocent people are going to get hurt. A lot of damage is going to be done on property.

SAM: Okay. Thank you, sir.

POLICEMAN: Right.

Street interview by Sam Walker, age 12. A few days after a confrontation between black high school students and police outside the Philadelphia Public Schools administration building, a group of black junior high students used battery-powered recorders to tape the reactions of passers-by in the predominantly white neighborhood surrounding their school. Note especially how Sam becomes increasingly articulate during the hour of recording and how he thinks on his feet to come up with a euphemism for "police brutality" when he finds himself talking with a policeman.

pieces may call for lightness or irony. Usually the two kinds of stories are intermixed, making the task even more difficult. The newscaster must alternate "up" and "down" moods without seeming detached or unfeeling.

Tape a professional five-minute news show so it can be replayed for in-depth analysis. Have students break the program into its components: station identification, background music or sound effects, the date and time, the headlines, the lead story, the subordinate stories, sports and weather, the commercials, and perhaps a humorous wrap-up item.

Such analysis leads naturally to small-group productions of original news shows. One student can anchor the program, another can do the sports, a third the weather, a fourth the commercial (recall our discussion of commercials under "The Disc Jockey Show"). Others can handle behind-the-mike jobs like writing, directing, recording, and timing.

Younger and less fluent readers might invent bulletins adapted from fairy tales or neighborhood happenings. Able readers can prepare scripts based on newspaper and magazine articles, school events, or topics covered in class. To make history come alive, have students create "time travel" broadcasts—for example, the six o'clock news the day Columbus returned from the "new" world. Like newspaper stories, radio news items answer the five W's—who, what, where, when, and why—but are usually shorter and less detailed.

The Person-On-The-Street Interview

The lightweight, battery-powered tape recorder, available in both open-reel and cassette formats, makes it possible for even elementary school students to interview people throughout their neighborhood. We've seen kids collect amazingly authentic data on topics ranging from health care to international affairs.

Mastering the Technique. Novice interviewers, like novice anglers, often come back with little to show for their efforts. Or, somewhat comically, they end up being interviewed by the person they were trying to interview. It takes practice to be able to ask a good question, shut up, wait for a response, and follow up immediately with another question. The best way for kids to learn how to do this is to see and hear it done. Role-play the interviewer yourself by standing in front of the class with a recorder and questioning half a dozen students. Later, let the kids interview you and then each other.

Planning the Interview. While spontaneity is always part of street-interviewing, planning makes the activity work. Kids should know what they want

It takes practice to ask a good question, shut up, wait for a response, and follow up.

Jack's Coffee Shop	
SOUND 1:	Door opens (traffic in background)
SOUND 2:	Tinkly bell above door rings
SOUND 3:	General low hubbub of people eating
SOUND 4:	Voice: "Can I help you?"
SOUND 5:	Voice: "I'll have a hamburger and a coke."
SOUND 6:	Coin inserted in slot of pinball machine
SOUND 7:	Pinball rolling, various pinball machine noises
SOUND 8:	Voice: "Ah, shoot!"
SOUND 9:	Rock music starts
SOUND 10:	Voice: "Check, please."
SOUND 11:	Cash register being rung up
SOUND 12:	Change being dropped into hand
SOUND 13:	Door opens, outside traffic is heard fade out

Sound essay by a Philadelphia junior-high teacher.

to find out. It's a good idea to have them write questions down before going out with the tape recorder. During the interview itself, however, kids should not read from notes.

Overcoming Shyness. Many kids are shy about approaching strangers. The answer is simple: don't start with strangers. Your students should first interview members of other classes, then other teachers, and finally people in the real world. It's also wise to send out two-person teams, since these odds make approaching a stranger less formidable. As an additional encouragement, point out that people are generally quite flattered to be asked their opinions. It's amazing how most adults will converse openly and at length with a tiny third grader, as if Walter Cronkite himself were behind the mike.

Handling Nasty People. The way to handle nasty people is not to. Teach your students to beat a polite and hasty retreat if someone tells them to bug off. Here again, in-class simulation—the teacher role-playing a grump—will prepare kids for the realities of reality.

Controlling Unwanted Background Noise. Most cities and towns are nosier than we realize. Our ears turn off the ambience, but the tape recorder won't. Cars, airplanes, echoes, even wind can drown out the interviewee's voice. The trick is to keep the mike no more than a foot from the speaker's mouth.

Editing. Every recorded interview is bound to include garbage. It is possible, of course, to edit out the unwanted material by splicing or re-recording the tape. But even during the recording process, the interviewer should consider switching the recorder off during obviously unproductive moments. This is a simple procedure if the mike has a remote-control switch.

Following Up. Tape recorded interviews can be used as resource material for oral or written reports, as part of a news program, or as the soundtrack for a film or slide-tape.

The Sound Essay

If nature abhors a vacuum, she also seems to have little use for silence. The swamp and the supermarket alike can be characterized by the sounds that fill their air.

The sound essay is the radio form most difficult to explain in words. You'll have to listen to recordings like the classic *An Evening in Sapsucker Woods* or the *Environments°* series to appreciate fully the narrative power of natural sound. Some sound essayists prefer to omit all verbal description and include only the sounds you'd hear if you were there. Of course, in many environments, human conversation is a natural sound.

A less pure, see-it-yourself version of the sound essay is the "walking-tour tape." Such recordings contain a sequential itinerary of a city, zoo, park, museum, or neighborhood. The person using the tape physically moves from place to place, carrying a battery-operated recorder. Upon reaching a particular destination, the tourist starts the recorder and looks at the attraction while the tape supplies background information. Note that our sample walking-tour script, written and performed by sixth graders, lacks visual detail since the producers assume the audience is looking while listening.

Another variation on the sound essay is the "time capsule." One of America's premier sound artists, Tony Schwartz, created one in which his niece grows from a crying baby to a young adult in only two minutes. The tape consists of snippits recorded each year over a span of fifteen years.°

For a less epic experience with time encapsulation, each of your students can record personal observations on his or her own cassette tape throughout the school year. The recording might include singing, philosophizing, memories, talks with friends, reactions to world news, thoughts on marriage, money, the future. At the end of the year, the tape can be entrusted to parents or otherwise stored for nostalgia and self-understanding.

Standards

The authors once judged a student radio tape contest. The range of entries was fantastic—everything from comedy shows to sound essays. That was encouraging. What was distressing was the lack of quality control. Some of the tapes could have been served up as the main event at a torture festival.

We speculated that many of the worst entries had never been listened to, even by the kids who made them. Maybe they thought getting the record-volume needle to wiggle was enough. It wasn't.

This suggests a basic rule. Kids should listen carefully to their radio works and study the reactions of their audiences. Here are a few of the pitfalls we listened for, plus suggestions on how to avoid them.

Rambling. One tape in our sound contest consisted of two boys telling each other a few stale moron jokes, banging the mike and asking each other "Whatcha wanna talk about next?" This "production" left the judges wishing the tape, if not the kids, would self-destruct. Improvisation à la Mort Sahl and Jean Shepherd is probably the hardest kind of radio to bring off. It takes years of practice. For most kids, the antidote to rambling is careful pro-

---

Voice 1:   THE GREAT FLOOD
               OF BRANCHVILLE

Voice 2: The summer of 1955 brought drought to Branchville and Sussex County. It was not a new experience, but that year the drought had been worse than usual. By July 15th there was scarcely a blade of grass to be seen.

Early in August it began to rain. One shower followed another. The drought was broken. August the 18th saw rains of firehose force come to Branchville....

You will go from school to the center of town. Then go up Main Street to the funeral home. Go to your left, follow Kemah Lake Road, and stop on the first bridge. Look up-stream.

Voice 3: TURN OFF THE RECORDER UNTIL EVERYBODY CAN SEE UP-STREAM.

Voice 4: We are now talking about the upper dam of 1892. The upper dam stored the water to make electricity. In 1955 this dam was always open but branches clogged the dam and the water began to make a pond. Finally the dam broke. That is how the town got flooded.

Now cross the road and look down stream. You will see Turner's house.

Voice 3: TURN OFF THE RECORDER UNTIL EVERYONE CAN SEE TURNER'S HOUSE.

Voice 4: The bridge that used to be here broke off and went in front of Turner's house. The house wasn't flooded as much as all the others because of the bridge....

Walking-tour tape script by sixth graders at the Branchville School of Branchville, New Jersey.

gram planning, which means creating and rehearsing a written script before turning on the tape recorder.

Background Noise. Unwanted talk or noise can ruin the mood and believability of a radio program. Try to provide students with a quiet recording area (a rare facility in most schools). The optimal room is large enough to hold one or two tape recorders, a record player, a sound effects table, and several people, but it is not so large that echoes and ambience predominate. Look for something cozy and, if possible, fitted out with rugs and curtains. Remember this generalization: The conditions under which an audio recording is made will influence the sound quality just as much as the equipment used to make it.

Poor Miking. There is a world of difference between what the human ear hears during a recording session and what the microphone hears (and, consequently, what actually ends up on the tape). When they make radio plays, children often display complete ignorance of this principle, arranging themselves around the microphone as if it were a magic wand that can pick up sound waves from all directions at once. The result is that only a few of them sound appropriately "on mike," while characters who are supposed to be "right there" in the middle of the scene sound like they're on the moon.

If you have only one microphone and if like most mikes it picks up a voice well only when the performer is directly in front of it (a uni-directional mike), then it will be impossible for more than two or three kids to stand "on mike" at one time. Thus, they will have to continually jockey for position during the recording, being careful not to shuffle their feet (they can remove their shoes) or rattle their scripts.

Most children, even in the primary grades, can handle such maneuvering, although any group will contain a few who are so shy or concentrating so hard on their lines that nothing can convince them to take the long walk up to the mike when their cues arrive. The opposite personality is the "mike hog," the actor who is never willing to relinquish the spotlight of the mike's live area. Have him play The Sphinx.

Students must also avoid making mike noise. Location recordings like person-on-the-street interviews present a real problem here. Nonprofessionals should practice recording on-the-go tapes while holding the microphone as still as possible. Wind noise can be reduced by making a "wind screen" for the mike out of cardboard or foam rubber.

Poor Mixing. If you have a stereo tape recorder or a microphone mixer, you can employ several mikes simultaneously, as in professional radio production.

Collar for mike
Cardboard baffle
Cut hole in foam rubber ball

A microphone wind screen cuts down on unwanted noise when you are recording outside.

However, this luxury carries its own pitfalls, particularly when it comes to "balancing" voices against music held behind them. Nothing annoys a radio audience more than music which drowns out important dialogue, yet novice sound engineers are more likely to make this mistake than they are to hold the music too low. It's really quite impressive how effectively a faint, almost inaudible music track will register in the minds of listeners.

Level Fluctuation. Second cousin to the thumbscrew is the loud-soft-loud-soft routine which results when someone fiddles with the record level or when an actor suddenly moves closer to or further from the mike. One solution is to use a recorder with an automatic level control, but it's better for kids to learn to control their "mike posture."

Uncomfortable Acting. Because sane people in our culture are expected not to talk to themselves, students often become inhibited when recording their own voices. This is not a big problem with radio drama, since the actors can play off each other. For monologues, songs, news broadcasts, and other solos, it can help to have a live audience present, or at least to imagine an audience. Some professional performers believe they connect best when they envision and play to a single listener rather than "the public" or "the mass audience."

Distortion. When the record volume is set too high during a taping session, the resulting fuzzy sound is called "distortion." The opposite mistake—too low a record level—can be partially corrected by turning the volume up high during playback, but then you get flat sound and tape hiss. Distorted sound may also result from speaking too close to the mike or from a faulty patch cord during electronic editing.

Unlabeled Reels. This is more common than any technical or aesthetic error. We could program a week of *Inner Sanctum* with horror stories about the consequences of not labeling radio tapes. At the very least, the front of the box should be labeled. We also endorse marking the back of the box, the spine of the box, and the leaders on both ends of the tape. When it comes to identifying an unlabeled radio show, not even The Shadow knows.

Sources and Resources

1. Stan Freberg's giant sundae routine is on an album called *Freberg Underground—Show No. 1* (Capitol SM-2551).

2. A recording of some great radio commercials is included inside a book about advertising called *Creativity in Communications* (Greenwich, CT: New York Graphic Society, 1971).

3. The following collectors offer vintage radio plays (drama and comedy) on tapes and discs. These recordings often have flat tone and weak, fluctuating signals, so don't get cassette copies unless your machine has a good amplifier and a big speaker:

Radio Reruns, P.O. Box 724, Redmond, WA 98052; Radiola, Box H, Croton-on-Hudson, NY 10520; Sights and Sounds of America, Inc., Box 616, Nassau, DE 19969; Remember Radio, Inc., P.O. Box 2513, Norman, OK 73069; Golden Age Radio, P.O. Box 8404, St. Louis, MO 63132.

4. *An Evening in Sapsucker Woods* is part of Cornell University's Library of Natural Sounds. Write to the Cornell Laboratory of Ornithology, 33 Sapsucker Woods Road, Ithaca, NY 14850. The *Environments* series is put out by Atlantic Records, 1841 Broadway, New York, NY 10023.

5. Samples of Tony Schwartz's sound work may be heard on *Sounds of Children* (Folkways 5583) and *Sounds of My City* (Folkways 7341).

In 1872, Leland Stanford, wealthy governor of California, made a bet with an acquaintance that a racehorse in action sometimes has all four legs off the ground. He settled the question by getting the photographer, Eadweard Muybridge, to help him line up twenty-four still cameras, each one triggered by threads stretched across the horse's path. Thus, one of the world's first "movies" was a piece of authentic, real-world research of the sort we believe can occur when media and kids get together.

Other breakthroughs followed. Perforated film advanced by sprockets enabled experimenters to reduce the number of cameras to one and the number of horses to zero. Transparent film meant the movie could be projected on a screen instead of shown in toys like the Zootrope. Each separate picture came to be called a *frame*. The frames were photographed and projected so rapidly that the eye saw them as continuous motion.

By the turn of the century, all the technical problems were solved. Humankind's ancient dream of capturing and reproducing the movement of life had become a reality. It was now the task of pioneer filmmakers to take that reality and turn it into an art.

Concepts

Teachers often ask us how film illusions are created. They wonder, do you have to be a Hollywood wizard to shoot scenes on Saturn or stories involving cartoon characters? Happily, you don't. Like stage magic, most film tricks are easy to figure out—and duplicate—once you understand the medium's underlying concepts.

For example, in a recent low-budget war picture called *The Destruction of Devil's Castle*, a Nazi fortress is blown up. The fortress was really a model, less than seven inches high. By placing the model on a hill and shooting up at it, the camera operator was able to omit cues that might suggest its actual size. By switching back and forth from the model collapsing to actors running through a concrete tunnel, the film editor was able to create the illusion of saboteurs escaping an exploding fortress.

The four eighth graders who made *The Destruction of Devil's Castle* were not film prodigies. They were enthusiastic students with a script they liked. But armed with suggestions from their teachers and super-8 movie equipment from their school system's Instructional Materials Center they made the medium work for them. Your kids can do the same.

Scripting

Some of the best professional movie scripts border on the unreadable. This is inherent in their attempt to communicate in print what are really parallel, simultaneous aspects (dialogue, camera placement, mood, actions) of a single moment in the movie. The implication for amateurs is that their scripts need not flow with the orderliness and formality of a good "composition." What counts is whether the writers have worked out and recorded their ideas for the

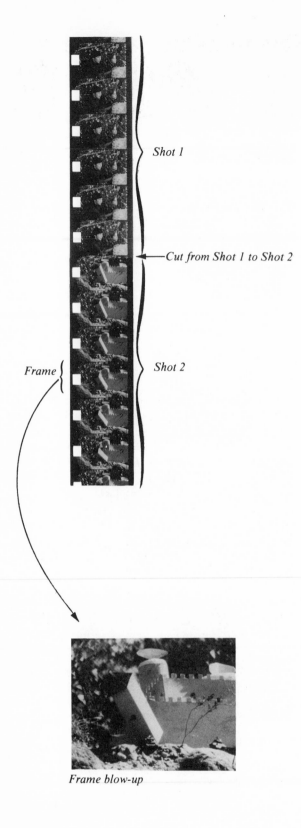

Shot 1

Cut from Shot 1 to Shot 2

Frame {

Shot 2

Frame blow-up

Toppling tower from student film, The Destruction of Devil's Castle, *produced by John Walker, Bob Wilder, Jim Waldron, and Steve Wojcik.*

film in a print form that they themselves can follow and use.

In the case of many documentaries, of course, no complete script is prepared ahead of time, but there will be notes on what people, objects, or happenings to shoot. After the filming, a structure for the documentary, including text for the narrator, is usually planned on paper.

A filmmaker may redraft a screenplay dozens of times before he or she is satisfied with it, and a number of outside authors may be imported to add their assorted touches. In the midst of all this effort, it is important to remember that while movies invariably rest on their scripts, they do not consist of them. The goal is not to translate dispassionately the script from paper to film but, rather, to *direct* it, which sometimes implies rejecting, adding, and rewriting material even as the picture is being shot. As director John Huston once remarked, there comes a time on every film project when you "throw away the script and make the movie."

Shooting

The basic unit of film language is not the scene but the *shot.* A shot is a series of consecutive frames recorded in one uninterrupted running of the camera. A movie is the sum of its individual shots. Frame blow-ups from several different shots in *The Destruction of Devil's Castle* appear on the next page.

The Set-Up. A "set-up" in filmmaking is the selected camera position from which a particular shot is taken. "Doing a set-up" is time-consuming and taxing. The camera must be picked up and carried to the next angle called for in the shooting script. The lights must be realigned, the composition rearranged, and the actors' movements rerehearsed while the director makes sure everything looks right from the camera's new viewpoint.

It's a good idea to take all the shots needed from a given set-up at one time. For example, suppose the shooting script looks like this:

Shot 1: Eugene standing on corner of Currier and Ives, waiting for Aaron. He looks at his watch.

Shot 2: Aaron getting into his car. Attacked by alligator. Delayed.

Shot 3: Eugene, still on the corner, gets tired of waiting. Leaves.

It would be most efficient to take Shot 3 immediately after Shot 1, while you are still in the right set-up, and order the shots correctly in the editing.

The Close-Up. While many different spatial relationships can occur between a camera and its subject, designated by terms like "low-angle" and "long-shot," one stands above the others: the "close-up." Perhaps the fundamental problem of photographing a movie is deciding what details are significant enough to shoot in close-up. A failing of many amateur filmmakers is that they either don't use close-ups or else use them haphazardly. We are not advocating close-ups *per se*. Many great directors employ close-ups sparingly, but those they do use count.

One memorable way to appreciate close-ups is to look at some very early silent shorts, especially those made between 1898 and 1907. These films are not only fun to watch, but clearly demonstrate how movie pioneers thought mainly in theatrical terms. The camera in an Edison comedy like *Laughing Gas* just sits there, front-row center, not doing much of anything except taking movies. But by 1911, directors had figured out how to apply close-ups in the middle of a scene to make the story more involving, as you can see by screening films like *The Lonedale Operator* and *The Battle of Elderbush Gulch*.°

The Zoom. Many modern movie cameras come equipped with zoom lenses. Through variable optical magnification, these lenses change the apparent camera-subject distance, thus enabling the filmmaker to nab a variety of shots—close-up, mid-shot, long-shot—from the same basic set-up. This becomes a special blessing when one is on a tight shooting schedule.

Zoom lenses also permit the camera operator to "zoom in" from a long-shot to a close-up while the camera is running. Like hot pepper, this technique should be applied with caution. Arbitrary, purposeless zooming is the hallmark of home movies, low-budget television films, and lackluster *cinéma-verité* documentaries. Many of our better film directors avoid zooming within a shot in favor of the kind of visual dynamics they can achieve only by actual camera movement or by "cutting" from one carefully composed set-up to the next.

Cutting

Like icons in the night, drive-in movie images rise to haunt our wanderings. Passing them on expressways, wishing we could stop to watch, we are attracted not only by the primitive power of the moving image but by the sense of dramatic progression from one shot to the next. A filmmaker refers to these abrupt changes between shots as *cuts*.

Uncut film, fresh from the laboratory, is called "rushes" or "dailies." The editor's job starts with questions about each shot in the rushes. Should the shot be used in the movie at all? On which frame

Long-shot

Mid-shot

Close-up

High-angle shot

Low-angle shot

should the shot begin? On which frame should it end? What shot should follow it? The answer to this last question—the question of whether two given shots will "cut together"—depends on the editing technique used for the cut: inter-cutting, match-cutting, or jump-cutting.

Inter-cutting. Inter-cutting is the least troublesome sort of film editing because the subject changes completely from one shot to the next. The three frame blow-ups on this page are from a scene in *The Destruction of Devil's Castle* in which an engineer trying to start his locomotive is inter-cut with a Nazi interfering with that intent.

Chase sequences are classic examples of the technique, as when Car No. 1, containing a man who has just sold the Verrazano Narrows Bridge, is inter-cut with Car No. 2, containing a man who has just bought it. One important concept in making such a scene work is "screen direction." If the salesman's car is moving across the screen from left to right in a particular shot, the next shot should show the customer's car also moving left to right. Otherwise, the cut might convey the confusing impression that the customer had suddenly given up and was headed the other way.

Match-cutting. In a match-cut, the same subject stays on the screen, and the cut reveals all or part of it from a new angle or distance. The term "match" implies continuity from one shot to the next. In a well-made match-cut, no gross portion of the subject's actual movement is omitted. For example, the cut illustrated on the next page—from the long-shot of the saboteur and guard to the close-up of the saboteur's pistol—would not seem nearly so smooth if in the second shot the pistol were pointed down.

Jump-cutting. As with match-cutting, jump-cutting implies keeping the same subject on the screen from one shot to the next, but there is no smooth continuity of action. The effect can be intriguing or atrocious.

Home movies are typically drenched with bad jump-cuts: people popping randomly around the screen, tiny bits of time thoughtlessly exterminated because the camera operator took his finger off the button for a split second, or camera-subject distances changed so slightly that they accomplished no effect beyond irritating the eye.

Good jump-cuts, made with intention and understanding, reduce running time, omit portions of the action not intrinsic to intelligibility, and keep up the pace. For example, if the movie is about a day in the life of a fortune cookie fortune-writer, the first shot might show her leaving a house and walking to a car. In the very next shot, she is shown in the car driving to work, trying to think up fortunes. Then there is a cut to her banging away at a typewriter. We are just as glad not to have to sit through her opening the door of the car or walking into the office, and the jumps are sufficiently extreme and dynamic that they do not come across as errors.

Recording

Silent movies were never really silent. There was always a piano or organ in the house. The initial runs of *The Birth of a Nation, Potemkin*, and many other spectaculars were accompanied by an orchestra playing a score composed especially for the films themselves. And, of course, there were subtitles, which many people acted out in their own heads and heard in their mind's ear.

The "coming of sound" in 1927 was not so much the coming of sound as the coming of soundtracks— the technology required for lip-synchronized singing and talking. All the "sound images" we discussed earlier as vital to radio now became available to film: voices, music, sound effects, ambience, and silence.

Sounds can absolutely transform a movie. Clinkety music makes slapstick more outrageous. Eerie chords enhance horror. Natural sounds may add to a film's realism or, when distorted—the magnified beating of the hero's heart—create symbolic or surreal ideas. Words spoken as dialogue can be intrinsic to the drama of a film. As narration, they clarify and extend the images.

While the technology for recording, synchronizing, editing, and mixing sounds is beyond the means of most amateur filmmakers, satisfactory ways exist for the home movie user to tap the potential of music, noises, narration, and even dialogue. At the very least, he can play a disc or tape of selected background music. Dialogue recording is discussed in the Activities section under "The Genre Film."

Acting

Since most audiences become more involved with a film's story and characters than they do with its photography and editing, it is high folly for a moviemaker to neglect anything that has to do with actors. This includes the costumes they wear, the sets and props they interact with, and, of course, the lines they say.

Film acting differs from stage acting in that it is done piecemeal. The actors must constantly stop and wait while the camera is moved to the next set-up or the film company is moved to the next shooting location. The director plays a crucial role here in maintaining consistency of characterization.

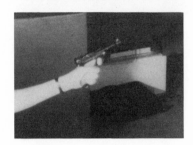

An abandoned locomotive becomes an "actor" in The Destruction of Devil's Castle.

The performance of dialogue in movies is closer to radio speaking than to stage speaking since the target is a microphone, not a distant ear in the balcony. The great danger is overacting.

Costuming, including make-up, ranks among the chief occupiers of "screen space," every square foot of which the filmmaker must worry over. Even the most ordinary clothes are never chosen carelessly. Consideration is given to each garment's relevance to a characterization and to the way it will photograph. Make-up, too, must be precisely applied lest it appear artificial under the scrutiny of the camera's lens.

Finally, there are the props. Because film has the unique capacity to focus all our visual attention on a single object—the cut to the knife glinting in the sunlight, the sudden closeup of the vampire's teeth—props are really a kind of actor in themselves. Hitchcock's *Frenzy*, for example, is remarkable for the impact it derives from stickpins, potatoes, neckties, and bowls of soup.

Although acting is as rich and complex a dimension of film as scripting, shooting, cutting, and sound recording, there are really only two mistakes an actor can never get away with. Most beginners know what they are. Walk onto the set of a student movie and right before the director says "action" you will probably hear the timeless refrain: "Don't look at the camera and don't break up."

Activities

In the good old days of un-super, regular 8mm, when one of the authors was in junior high school, he and his friends were inspired to make a horror movie. We wrote a script, gathered our Halloween masks together, stuck candles all over the attic, and started shooting. The result was titled *The Monster-Maker*.

We told our ninth-grade English teacher how we'd been spending our weekends, and she invited us to show *The Monster-Maker* in class. It was such a big hit that the audience chipped in their lunch money to start us on a new film, and before long we had formed our own company. We called this enterprise Abington-International Movie Company because we all lived in Abington Township, Pennsylvania, and because International sounded important.

And to us the whole thing *was* important. We agonized over technical flaws and unreliable machines, hoarded every penny we took in at the box office (*Calliostro the Sorcerer* was a smash hit with the little kids in the neighborhood), made posters and handbills inspired by Hollywood posters and handbills, and more than once tangled with adult authority.

The most memorable such adventure occurred because the script for our first comedy, *The Man Who Owned America*, called for a shot of the President and his aide running through the gates of the White House. We went to Washington, set up our camera on the pavement in front of the Treasury Building, and started our actors running through the gates of the White House. In the middle of the first take the Secret Service materialized and dragged us to an untraveled section of the White House grounds, convinced that they were foiling evil designs upon President Johnson. But after we carefully explained that the production was for real, that we were a reputable concern with a half-dozen previous pictures behind us, they let us go with a bemused "Good luck."

Moviemaking for us was a total experience that went way beyond shooting up film for the fun of it. Rehearsing bits of comedy or horror, sewing costumes together, testing make-up ideas for *Revenge of the Monster-Maker*, building model war machines for *The Futurians* (invaders from the year 2000), getting reluctant actors to say their lines without breaking up, discovering the dynamics of tilting the camera and shooting at weird angles (and then proceeding to overuse the technique shamelessly)—these were all challenging but cherished parts of the deal.

We believe this kind of richness is inherent in the activities that follow. Even the simplest of them involves the issues of scripting, acting, prop gathering, set planning, and visual thinking that made Abington-International Movie Company tick.

Student actors tempt adult authority to get an exciting shot for The Man Who Owned America.

The One-Reeler

The length of a silent movie was often advertised in terms of how many "reels" it ran. One reel lasted ten minutes. Thus, a "two-reel comedy" was twenty minutes long, a "three-reeler" was a half hour.

Today this terminology is no longer used. Instead, producers talk of "feature length" (100 minutes on average) or TV length (28½ or 57 minutes). For most amateurs, such lengths are both economically impossible and artistically unnecessary. By returning to the concept of the one-reel short, the student moviemaker can save film and money, yet tell a story that has the scope and feel of a feature.

Super-8 cameras use cartridges containing slightly over three minutes of film (50 feet). If you give yourself a two-to-one shooting ratio (that is, if you shoot two feet of film for each one you include in the final movie), you can film and edit a super-8 one-reeler for about $30.00. This budget includes six cartridges

Most good documentaries are propaganda films. This does not mean they tell lies.

(20 minutes worth) and their processing, as well as two packs of splicing tapes. Thus, Jules Feiffer's goal for comic books—"movies on paper"—is no longer the imperative it was when he stated it. Today, a Jules Feiffer would not have to grow up before he could make a real movie.

One-reel filmmaking can concretize any curriculum. We have seen original classroom shorts ranging from an account of Joseph and his Coat of Many Colors, produced for a Bible-as-Literature class, to a dramatic biography of Galileo, produced for a science class. In a humanities class, of course, student one-reelers do not communicate specific knowledge so much as they communicate the director's likes, dislikes, story ideas, or dreams.

The Documentary

A documentary film presents the real-life story of a person, institution, or event. While many modern documentary filmmakers rely heavily on extended shots of people talking, kids can certainly engage this form without having "synch sound" equipment. Narration and music may be recorded on a separate tape or dubbed onto a print or final cut of the film. Subjects for school documentaries might include how food is prepared in the cafeteria, the behavior of people waiting for a bus, conflict on the playground, what the local incinerator looks like in operation, or a day in the life of a traffic cop.

An economics or business administration class could even try going into the "documentary business." The idea here is for kids to hire themselves out to a neighborhood birthday party, cook-out, or wedding to make a film of the event. When the traditional "home movie" is reconceived as a "home documentary," the results are often much more pleasing to everyone involved—the difference between making movies and simply taking movies.

Three problems recur in classroom documentary production. The first is underexposed film. Without artificial lights, super-8 color film shot indoors almost never turns out bright enough. Setting up lights at a documentary location can be extremely difficult for the filmmaker and distracting for the subject. Therefore, you should almost always use a relatively "fast" black and white film, such as Kodak's Tri-X, and even then you should try to shoot in rooms containing a healthy amount of "available light" (fluorescent room lights or daylight coming in through the windows).

This is not to imply that black and white is a handicap. Indeed, one of the biggest problems facing the documentarian is the enormous quantity of irrelevant, chaos-inducing detail that clutters most environments. Among these details are colors. Black and white photography can add the virtue of simplicity to a film, and great documentaries like *Olympia*, *Hospital*, and *Man of Aran* would probably lack much of their classic, almost symbolic austerity if their images contained splashes of bright color. (For weddings, parties, and similarly festive events, though, color carries a special appeal and is worth the headaches of artificial lighting.)

The second problem is stilted or unnatural action. Shots of people slinking away from the camera or, conversely, attacking it with idiotic grins communicate nothing except that the filmmaker has failed to relax his subject. It helps to give your performer simple tasks: "Trim this rose." "Okay, blow out the candles." "Let me get you flipping the hamburger again." Play down the mystique of moviemaking. Don't come on like a Hollywood crew. Explain your equipment and what kinds of shots you need. Finally, be prepared to waste a bit of film while the subject warms up to the camera.

The third problem is uninspired ideas. Confronted with the documentary format for the first time, at least half of your students will decide to make a film about "the school." The trouble is that only a master documentarian can pull together so diverse an institution as "the school." A more manageable project for novices might be "the playground" or "the track team" or even "the school on Saturday afternoon." By concentrating on a limited aspect of his subject, the student is more likely to make a real statement.

To give another example, one of the authors once supervised a documentary by some eleventh graders about a McDonald's hamburger shop. The footage turned out fine technically, but the movie itself had no idea behind it. It didn't document a particular event at McDonald's or show us things you wouldn't normally see there. All we got were shots of orders being filled, money changing hands, and people eating, with no controlling concept relating one image to the next.

Most good documentaries are propaganda films. This does not mean they tell lies. It means they leave us with no doubts about whether the filmmaker regards his material with compassion, contempt, or something in between.

The Instructional Film Loop

Kids who can take or leave most professionally made super-8 loops often react with genuine enthusiasm when invited to make their own. The finished product, a two or three minute film that plays over and over again in a special cartridge, makes for a dandy display at an open house or an educational fair.

Science topics in particular lend themselves to loop production. Stunning results can be obtained using "time-lapse" photography to speed up processes normally too slow to observe: plants or crystals growing, flowers opening, clouds transmuting. To get the effect, lock the camera securely on a tripod; frame the subject; expose the film intermittently, two or three frames at predetermined intervals, making sure the light is held constant each time.

Film loops are one of those media projects in which the results often compare favorably with the output of commercial companies. Because the form focuses on a single visual idea, the problems of sound, dramatic acting, and multiple camera set-ups are all avoided or reduced. Often the teacher is the writer-director, scripting the film to fulfill a specific need in the curriculum. The students function as co-authors, crew members, and on-camera performers.

Incidentally, the cost of a school-made loop is generally several dollars less than the cost of a commercially produced one. Your budget, beyond the expected outlay for film, developing, and splices, should include having the movie mounted in a cartridge, a service your IMC's hardware suppliers will do for less than $5.00. Note: Since super-8 loops are part of the Great Black Box Conspiracy described in Chapter 2, you are advised to mount a duplicate print of your movie in the cartridge, rather than the camera original. Otherwise, you risk losing your "master" film to a malfunctioning projector, especially if the footage has splices in it.

The Genre Film

Some children have trouble thinking up ideas for movies. One strategy is for them to focus on a particular genre which excites them. The range is rich: mystery, war, western, horror, slapstick, swashbuckler, serial, science fiction, secret agent, soap opera, superhero/superheroine, fantasy, crime, animal, motorcycle, jungle, detective, melodrama, martial arts.

Adults sometimes express dismay when they see children's films that are patent imitations of the made-for-television variety. Our own position, suggested in Chapter 2, is that frankly influenced but

Time-lapse photography reveals the growth of plants (top) in a high school student's film loop.

Horror is an ever popular genre. This apparition (center) appears in the student film, Calliostro the Sorcerer.

The comedy genre, exemplified by The Man Who Owned America *(bottom), invites bravura acting.*

Ray gun trick (top) from an 8mm homage to Star Trek *by John Walker, age 14.*

Parachute stunt (center) from The Destruction of Devil's Castle *has a tiny "GI Joe" doll standing in for a teenage actor.*

Artificial snow (bottom) adds to a sailor's agonies in The Ancient Mariner, *an adaptation of Coleridge's poem by tenth graders George Shelps and Jim Morrow.*

enthusiastic production can be an important step toward genuine creativity. And even the most derivative *Dracula* frequently demands sophisticated problem-solving: translating an idea from print to film, finding the right camera angle, getting actors and crew to work cooperatively.

Genre movies provide an opportunity for kids to experiment with special effects. Five of the more startling tricks are:

Appearing and Disappearing. Place the camera on a tripod. Film the action up to an appropriate point —say, a sorcerer gestures at a jar of peanut butter— then stop the camera, move the peanut butter out of the frame (but the sorcerer must stay "frozen"), and start shooting again. In the film, the peanut butter will suddenly pop off the screen. Reverse the procedure to have the peanut butter reappear.

Death Rays. With a thin but sturdy pin you can make rays appear to come out of the barrels of space guns or the eyes of invaders by scratching into the emulsion (dull) side of the developed film. Given the small frame size, a magnifying glass is required for this operation. The scratches should be repeated for a dozen frames or so to show up clearly on projection.

Sky Full of Stars. Make pin pricks of various sizes in a large black sheet of paper and light it from behind (with a "movie light," window light, light table, etc.). Model space ships can be glided across it on black strings. When you light the space ships, however, keep reflections off the black paper, or it will look like black paper instead of deep space.

Giants and Dwarfs. There are many ways to disguise the actual size of a film subject. Carefully framed, a miniature prop will look gigantic. This trick can turn a toy train into a real locomotive, or a gerbil into a city-wrecking monster.

Rain and Snow. Filmmakers, unlike the general populace, do something about the weather. Rainmaking is simple. Stage the scene against a broad backdrop, such as a hedge or the side of a building, to avoid revealing good weather in the distance. Have an off-camera assistant spray water in a high arc from one or more garden hoses. Indoors, frame a window in the shot and direct the spray against it from the outside. For snow, you need lots of soap flakes and at least two assistants sprinkling it from ladders or upper story windows.

In conceiving genre films, students often want to have the actors say lines of dialogue. "Live sound," recorded on the set, is not possible with most home movie equipment. There is no way to stop or start a tape recorder at the exact same time as the camera, and even if you could you would lose synchronization because of variations in the motors' speeds. Professionals solve the problem by transmitting an electronic synch pulse, either by radio or over a cable, from the camera to the tape recorder and by transferring the tape to sprocketed "magnetic film" and editing it as if it were movie film.

Dialogue can be added to a finished super-8 student movie in several ways. The classic method, still serviceable, is subtitles—words lettered neatly enough to be read easily, photographed long enough to be read slowly, and inserted into the visual flow of the film at appropriate points. Subtitles should be short, giving only the essence of the conversation. The audience will fill in.

Students bent on "real" sound can use the process known as "dubbing." This is easiest if you have a super-8 projector of the sort that permits you to record directly onto a magnetic stripe running along one edge of the film.

If you don't have a sound projector but you do have a fairly good open-reel tape recorder with "instant stop," then follow the procedure outlined below. It is rather perverse, however, and should be reserved for movies that cannot possibly get by with pantomime acting or subtitles. One given is that someone familiar with the film be present at all showings, continually making adjustments to keep picture and soundtrack in synch.

1. Shoot the movie with the actors saying the lines in the script as if their voices were being recorded.
2. Edit the film completely.
3. Have the actors watch the movie while trying to say their lines in correspondence to the lip movements on the screen. Sound effects and background music should be rehearsed at the same time.
4. Punch a hole in one frame of the film's leader and thread it up over the projector aperture. Put a dot on the leader of the tape with a magic marker and place it over the record head.
5. Start the machines and start the dub.
6. Do it over and over until you get a decent take.
7. Show the film back by lining up the cue marks as in Step 4 and again starting the machines together. (Don't worry about starting them at *precisely* the same time, though. Because of the imperfection of their motors, they will always go out of synch. Always.).
8. When the tape recorder gets ahead, flip the instant stop control for an instant. When the projector gets ahead, throw it into still for an instant.

A third approach to super-8 sound, barely tested in schools as this book goes to press, is the so-called

Subtitles enable student filmmakers to avoid the complexities of synchronized sound, as in these three successive shots (top) from Mick Owen, Boy *of the Future, a comedy by Rene Calvo, age 17.*

Behind the scenes (bottom): shooting the Mick Owen *subtitle in a high school media center.*

talkies system devised by Eastman Kodak. Here, sound is recorded directly onto an edge-stripe as the film cartridge is exposed in the camera. We encourage you and your students to invest in such hardware only after you know exactly what you'll be doing with it and what its limitations are. To quote ourselves, a medium is defined by its grammar, not by the latest technology.

The Cut-out Animation Film

When movie film is exposed only a few frames at a time instead of by a continuous running of the camera, the technique is called *animation* (also known as "single-frame" and "stop-motion"). Animation can be used to make inanimate things—model monsters, cartoon drawings, cut-out characters—come to life. "Cut-out" animation is the easiest and most versatile type to do with children.

After he writes his script, the student should prepare his backgrounds ("12 x 18" is a good size) and his characters (in scale to each other and to the backgrounds). Oaktag is the best material for the characters. It's flexible enough for children to cut with scissors and sturdy enough to resist warping and withstand "hinging" (with string or brass clips) of arms and legs. Magazine pictures can be turned into cartoon props, settings, and characters if the student cuts them up carefully and mounts them on cardboard.

Because the whole illusion of animation depends on the apparent movement of figures in relation to a static frame, it is essential to lock the camera on a tripod, ladder, or copy stand. The backgrounds should also be secured, either with masking tape or weights. The ideal camera for animation has five features:

A Focusing Scale. This is a series of numbers etched on the lens, making it clear how close the camera can be moved to the art work without losing focus. A 3-foot minimum is great because then the camera can be placed low enough for the children to look in the viewfinder without standing on chairs. More commonly, the minimum is 6 feet. If your camera has fixed focus instead of a focusing scale, keep it as far from the art work as possible and use a lot of light. You should get a relatively sharp image, but run a test first.

A Zoom Lens. Its virtue in amateur production is that once the minimum camera-subject distance is established, you can zoom in (without the camera running) and begin animating a close-up of part of the scene. If your camera does not have a zoom lens, the easiest way to do close-ups is simply to prepare additional large-scale cut-outs of heads, hands

holding props, and whatever other "larger than life" details the script suggests.

A Single-frame Release. This enables you to expose just one frame at a time. If your camera lacks this feature, you can click off between three and four frames by squeezing the motor-release button for a split second. However, this technique carries a high risk of moving the camera itself, so be certain to bolt it down rigidly.

A Reflex Viewfinder. This type of viewfinder shows exactly what the lens of the camera is seeing. Without this feature, close-up shots, including animation set-ups, often wind up annoyingly off-center. If your camera does not have through-the-lens viewing, consult the instructions for information on compensating for the disparity (parallax) between what the lens sees and what the viewfinder shows.

Exposure Lock. If your camera has an automatic exposure feature but not an exposure lock, you will get a flickery image—some of your frames will catch the electric eye in the process of readjusting for the hand that was there an instant ago manipulating the art work. To solve this problem, let a few seconds elapse between removing your hand and clicking off the frames, thus giving the electric eye time to return the diaphragm to the correct opening.

The biggest problem children have with animation is moving their cut-outs too much between exposures. They should get in the habit of moving the characters a half-inch or less each time, recording each new position by clicking off two successive frames—"on two's" as professional animators say. If in the finished film the kids find the art work flies by too quickly, they can try animating "on three's" next time.

The other common difficulty occurs when one child starts clicking off frames before the animator has removed his hand or head from the camera's view. These errors can be edited out, but it's best not to make them in the first place.

Some kids have deeper, more conceptual problems with animation. They seem not to realize that if a flying saucer is to travel from the mother ship on the left of the screen to the building on the right, they can't just pick it up and move it in one blow. Every action that is not actually *animated* will come out on the film as a confusing jump. After this concept is explained to them once or twice, most children catch on.

The first time they try animating, kids usually fall into the rigid frame of reference of the early movie pioneers. Be sure to remind them about the close-up, and the kind of excitement, clarity, and interest this technique can bring to a film. Close-ups are also a good way to cover mistakes. If somebody bumps the tripod way out of kilter while you're in the middle of animating a long-shot, you can cut to a close-up to avoid a bad jump-cut.

Cut-out animation is often applied to other categories of moviemaking, including the fiction genres, documentary (using pictures of famous people or events from books, magazines, and newspapers), and instructional "subject matter" films. The four frame blow-ups on this page, for example, come from a mathematics cartoon made by two seventh grade girls. It's called *Tips on Reducing*—all about a fraction who takes some hunger pills, does a few exercises, and manages to "reduce."

The Table-top Animation Film

Three-dimensional objects—toys, models, dioramas, lumps of clay—can be animated just like two-dimensional cut-outs. This kind of animation is generally more complicated than cut-out animation, but many students find that it is also more exciting and professional-looking, and we have seen third graders try it with reasonable success. It is called "table-top" animation because the objects to be animated are generally placed on a table, the more rigid the better.

The big problem with table-top animation is remembering which of the objects have already been moved for the upcoming exposure and which have not. If the animator's memory falters, the final film will include the chaotic effect of certain objects flying across the screen while others stay unnaturally immobile. One trick is to keep a running "character movement diary." Alternatively, assign a different person to be the animator of each object.

Perhaps the ultimate model-animator's nightmare was presented to Hollywood wizard Ray Harryhausen in the 1955 science-horror picture, *It Came From Beneath the Sea.* The It was a giant octopus. Harryhausen reduced the variables somewhat by giving his model only six tentacles instead of the traditional eight. As he predicted, only the octopi in the audience noticed.

Standards

Filmmaking will never be a very satisfying activity for you and your kids if you approach it as a "blockbuster," one-time-only experience. True, there is nothing like the excitement and romance of a first film. But the full potential of classroom movie production will be reached only when students start making lots of films, all the time, in groups that are neither unrealistically large nor impractically small.

Animated arithmetic (top) from Tips on Reducing, *a film by Pat Dzuris and Sharon Jones. The fraction 10/20 figures out how to reduce to 5/10.*

Six-armed octopus model (bottom) harasses San Francisco.

In *Breaking Through, Selling Out, Dropping Dead and Other Notes on Filmmaking*, William Bayer argues that film is a lousy medium for what is usually called "self-expression."° It does many things awfully well, but one thing it doesn't do is let you take ideas off the top of your head and put them directly into the form of a message. Whether the student's goal is as ambitious as getting his inner identity on film or as simple as making a time-lapse documentary about a bean, five common mistakes are worth worrying about.

Vague Ideas. Many ideas for films rely so much on imagery that reducing them to words does not do them justice. But there is a big difference between the filmmaker who is unable to do justice to her idea and the filmmaker who is unable to describe it in words at all. Student directors should get in the habit of sharing their scripts with friends, parents, or potential collaborators. The reactions of these people can be vital in shaping further drafts.

Technical Difficulties. Your camera's instruction booklet offers advice on avoiding underexposure, overexposure, unsharp focus, poor color, and bad framing (parallax problems). But even if you follow directions, technical catastrophe will still overtake a crucial shot or two. The answer is simple if hard to swallow: go back and shoot again. Your kids should understand that this is not an act of desperation or an admission of stupidity, but a normal procedure in every kind of filmmaking. Stanley Kubrick redid many of the special effects in his evolution epic, *2001: A Space Odyssey*, because the initial attempts were not convincing enough. Robert Flaherty had to return to the Far North and reshoot all of his famous documentary, *Nanook of the North*, because the original negative was destroyed in a fire.

Shotless Thinking. Experienced filmmakers think in terms of shots. They say to themselves, "First I'll need a long-shot of Cindy approaching the tree and grabbing the first branch. Then I'll take a close-up of her hands curled around the branch. Then I'll take a low-angle shot of her hoisting herself up. Then I'll climb the tree myself and get a high-angle shot of her as she comes up higher."

Instead of bothering with this kind of division into discrete, nameable shots, the novice typically shoots off the cuff, panning redundantly back and forth, zooming as the spirit moves him. As a remedy, we recommend that beginners work from a shot-by-shot script. Having the camera on a tripod can also help induce shot-consciousness.

Amateurs who do not realize that a movie can be broken down into separate shots also tend not to realize it is possible to *rehearse* a particular shot's content over and over until all the bugs are worked out, and none of this repetitiveness will register on film (or in the minds of the audience) as long as the camera motor is stopped. Kids who impetuously flick on the camera before the actors and crew know exactly what to do should be informed that this is the surest way to make the film turn out wrong. Of all the principles of movie production, none has more implications than the simple-minded notion that the camera "sees" only when it is exposing footage, and when it is not, the most outrageous sort of legerdemain can transpire before it.

The same idea applies to the difference between what is permissible within the borders of a shot and what is permissible just beyond them. It's amazing how, even with a low-budget movie, it is almost impossible to picture the tangle of lights, people, and bizarre hardware positioned just slightly off-screen. We know in our conscious thoughts that these things are there, but our imaginations are having too much fun to admit them.

Insufficient Coverage. Editing a professional movie is a mind-boggling endeavor. The rushes for the average feature are a vast, sprawling, highly redundant collection of scenes covered in their entirety from several different set-ups, each of which comprises one or more shots, each of which is covered by several different takes. The editor and the director must decide which shot presents the idea of the moment most powerfully, which parts of each take of a given shot play well (in terms of acting, overall feel, or simply absence of mistakes), and how to cut all the good material together while still maintaining a sense of continuity.

Editing an amateur film is generally less complicated. When there is a limit on available time, equipment, or know-how, some amateurs use the technique of "cutting in the camera"—holding each shot to one take and matching the action by having the actors "freeze" in place between shots or by filming "reaction shots" of characters watching the main action.

But if the project is ambitious, if you have a fair amount of time and film, and if a "viewer" with a bright screen is at your disposal, then you should shoot with the full resources of cutting in mind. If your script calls for a cut from an exterior view of someone entering a haunted house to the interior of the house as the door continues to open, you should film the action twice, once from the inside and once from the outside. In the editing, you can remove all redundant frames and make a good match-cut. The general principle is to shoot a lot of "coverage" for each scene, grabbing reaction shots, insert shots of props, and new angles on complete scenes, even if you are not certain how they might fit into the finished movie. Such material proves useful in the editing room for avoiding bad cuts and adding visual variety.

Squeamish Cutting. Just as a filmmaker should be shot-conscious when shooting, he or she should be frame-conscious when editing. If any doubt exists whether a bit of film—anything from a whole scene to a single frame that might be slowing down a match-cut—can come out without distressing the audience, then it should come out. There never was a film that was too short.

The most prolific species of unnecessary frame occurs between the time the camera is started and the time the actors catch on and begin acting. When cutting in the camera, the solution is to give the call for "action" first and the call for "camera" immediately afterwards. When cutting on an editing bench, omit every frame of the pause.

Beyond tricks of the trade, film editing involves a unique, almost primitive sense of power, the power of order wrought from chaos. In amateur movie production, this is especially felt when making the last splice, the splice that joins one reel of already-edited scenes to another. What was once a jumble of disconnected, unordered images has suddenly become a movie, a story, an argument about life. The last splice is one of the best moments in film, affirming that things can make sense when brains and fingers work together.

Sources and Resources

1. Early silent shorts are available in both super-8 and 16mm from Blackhawk Films, 27 Eastin-Phelan Building, Davenport, IA 52808. Particularly instructive are the Edison comedies, the Melies trick films, and the pre-Griffith Biograph shorts, as well as *The Great Train Robbery, The Lonedale Operator*, and the 1911 version of *Dr. Jekyll and Mr. Hyde*. Blackhawk also distributes an enlightening little short called *How to Make Home Movies Your Friends Will Want to See Twice*.

2. Yvonne Anderson's *Teaching Film Animation to Children* (New York: Van Nostrand Reinhold) remains the most complete discussion so far of cutout and table-top animation.

3. William Bayer's unorthodox thoughts on "self-expression in film" appear on pages 89-90 of *Breaking Through, Selling Out, Dropping Dead* (New York: Dell Publishing Company, 1971).

4. The best book on the technological realities of non-Hollywood, independent production is Edward Pincus's *Guide to Filmmaking* (New York: Signet Books, 1969).

5. Douglas Lowndes's *Film Making in Schools* was mentioned earlier as one of the few truly multimedia curricular guides around. It is also the strongest text on classroom movie production *per se*.

6. A "film grammar book" our parents like a lot is *Moviemaking Illustrated: The Comicbook Filmbook* by James Morrow and Murray Suid (Rochelle Park, NJ: Hayden Book Company, 1973).

Television: 9
Videotaping facts and fictions

The Medium Is The Messiah would be a good title for the history of technology in education. In recent years, televisionaries have foretold an era in which classroom TV will solve the reading problem, the teaching problem, and even the creativity problem. The rhetoric is entrancing and invigorating. It is also old.

Return with us now to those thrilling days of yesteryear when radio, not television, gripped the imaginations of children and teachers alike. In 1948, *Radio in Elementary Education* was just one of many manifestoes that predicted educational breakthroughs thanks to the (vacuum) tube. The argument was simple and direct: Because children in 1948 are habituated to radio, and because there are almost no limits to the content it can carry, the medium should be harnessed for improved in-school learning. Radio's ability to reach the average child right at his own classroom desk invites the broadcasting of "master lessons" by "master teachers," thereby infusing schools with a universally high level of instruction. At the same time, motivated by the opportunity to produce their own radio shows, children will automatically develop their communication skills to lofty levels of proficiency.

The revolution never happened. But *Radio in Elementary Education* will have justified the paper it was printed on if it reminds us to be humble in our claims for media.° Television in and of itself will not work miracles, nor will such highly touted offshoots as video-cassettes, video-discs, community antenna

(CATV), and non-figurative feedback. Like the hammer, the wax crayon, and, yes, the radio before it, TV is a tool that people can use to shape their world. And like every new tool, it needs less promotion and more understanding.

The first thing worth knowing about television is that it is not film. It's surprising how many educators still use the terms "film" and "television" or "filming" and "taping" interchangeably. Both media are evolving, and eventually they may become one and the same, but right now the differences matter. There are times when one of your kids will write a script that calls for a TV production, and times when only a movie will turn the trick.

Film was born of a desire to record movement and preserve it for later learning, appreciation, or entertainment. Television was born of a desire to broadcast movement (and accompanying sound) over great distances, so that people miles away from an event could see it while it was happening, in a manner analogous to the transmission of sound alone via radio.

The invention of videotape in 1955 brought TV and the movies closer together. Now television, too, was a medium for preserving images. But videotape still retains the here-and-now "presence" of live television, as opposed to the basically photographic feel of film. The images are not literally visible on the tape but must be "retrieved" electronically.

So much for theory. Suppose your school has sunk its savings into a mess of video equipment, in-

stead of a mess of movie equipment. Suppose, further, that the equipment is uncharacteristically not in the repair shop or about to go there. What can you expect from this hardware that you can't expect from film hardware? (In the rest of this chapter, we shall assume that your school system is working in the popular *half-inch* videotape format. Most of the ideas that follow apply equally to the *one-inch* format that a few schools have, and to the *three-quarter-inch cassette* format many will acquire in the future.)

1. Movie film has to be developed before you can look at it and figure out what needs to be retaken. With videotape, just rewind and sit back for an instant replay.

2. You can use a roll of movie film only once, whereas you can erase and re-record the same reel of half-inch videotape many times. (Eventually, scratches and deposits start building up on the tape and appearing on the screen as darting horizontal lines called "dropout.")

3. Sound with movies is a complicated business. Most amateurs don't even attempt the technology of "synch sound" recorded on the set along with the film. With videotape you get "synch sound" without even trying, for every videotape recorder is also an *audio*tape recorder.

There are, however, three distinct limitations to half-inch video as compared with movies.

1. You cannot do conventional animation with it.

2. Color in motion pictures is achieved in the software (film). Color in video is achieved in the hardware (cameras, recorders, receivers). Compared with black and white TV technology, color TV technology involves higher costs, more maintenance, and trickier lighting.

3. The individual shots in a movie can be endlessly reconsidered, rearranged, and retimed, yet, if splicing is done carefully, the cuts will not be distracting. The kind of editing you can do with your school's half-inch video system is not nearly so dynamic.

Videotape cannot be physically cut and spliced—not, at least, without creating dreadful distortions in the image and possibly damaging your equipment. With a battery-operated recorder, like Sony's famous "portapak," you can get away with a kind of "cutting in the camera" (see Chapter 8) by simply stopping the tape and then starting it again. However, such cuts have a high tendency to "break up" and give your show a choppy, disjointed feel. If you have a second recorder with an "edit" facility—Sony's 3650, for example—you can make cuts by re-

Strip of 16mm movie film (left) containing a very interesting arrangement of snorkles. Piece of half-inch videotape (right) containing a nude figure-skating team.

recording selected segments onto a new reel of tape, leaving out the dull parts and putting the good ones in the right order. Even then, the edits are likely to break up after repeated playing.

For these reasons, movie-like "quick cutting" is not feasible on most schools' videotape recorders. Instead, each section of tape to be re-recorded ought to be fairly long and continuous—a single, uninterrupted thirty-second shot taken with a portapak during a visit to a yo-yo factory, for example, to be followed by an uninterrupted forty-five seconds of the same students discussing and demonstrating contemporary yo-yo trends, taped in a studio. (This second section might have quite a few cuts already in it, if the particular studio had two cameras and the director did a lot of "switching" between them.) On the other hand, as primitive as half-inch video editing is, it shares with film editing the same wonderful ability to let you take separately created segments and fuse them into finished shows.

Concepts

Television is the only medium covered in this book whose first decade as a popular entertainment (roughly 1947-1957) corresponds to its so-called "golden age." Whether this was truly TV's golden age or whether that designation should be held in reserve is a question for the historians. But it certainly was an *exciting* age.

Early television was literally "live," but it was also live with possibility, with the sense of a medium in emergence. Here was the first visual communications form that could give immediacy and presence to remote happenings—anything from a news analysis by Edward R. Murrow to a comedy sketch by Sid Caesar to a new play by Paddy Chayefsky.

It was in the realm of drama, probably, that live television reached its apex. A special kind of obsessive, almost crazed effort was required to produce a live television play, to coordinate the technical complexities of cameras and microphones with the psychological complexities of acting and staging. When air time arrived, there was no turning back, no possibility of reversing an electronic or aesthetic miscalculation.

In the mid-Fifties, George Roy Hill staged what may have been the ultimate: an adaptation of Walter Lord's nonfiction thriller, *A Night To Remember*. To create the sinking of the Titanic, he employed 107 actors, 31 sets, and 7 cameras. Rather incredibly, Hill and company did the whole production over again five weeks later.

Something of the stimulating spontaneity of early television survives today in the small, easy-access studios now springing up across the country in cable stations, universities, and, of course, public school systems. Whether your school has a complete multiple-camera studio or simply a room with a portapak in it, five basic concepts will be involved in getting your productions onto the tube.

Program

A successful TV show begins, as a rule, not with an undifferentiated desire to "use video" but with a specific idea for a program. It's not enough simply to select a format (quiz program, talk show, documentary) or genre (western, detective, comedy, science fiction). The idea must be worked out, which might mean anything from writing narration to scouting locations to thinking up interview questions to preparing a full-dress script.

If the initial concept is "a documentary about the city park," for example, a professional TV crew would not simply pop over to the place and start spraying their camera around like a garden hose. Even if they arrive with no concrete notions in their heads—and much can be said for letting locations suggest a show's specifics—they spend time looking around, getting a feel for the place, and thinking. Then they decide that the unifying subject, the idea for the program, will be the grandmother who builds model aircraft carriers and sails them in the park's duck pond.

Coverage

Television directors speak of using their cameras to "cover" the subject at hand, whether the subject is a football game, The Uncle Bozo Show, or an obnoxious plug for mail order records.

Single-camera Coverage. In the eagerness to set up impressive-looking, hardware-loaded studios, media specialists sometimes underestimate the potential of portable, single-camera rigs. Portability opens up all kinds of production possibilities—one-act plays staged on subways, vocational guidance tapes made in factories and businesses, interviews with people in their "natural environments."

But even in a studio, single-camera coverage can be dynamic. Judicious zooming and panning (swiveling the camera), combined with some particular tricks of the trade, can impart a sense of "separate shots" to a show that was actually recorded from one set-up in one continuous rolling of tape. Indeed, as far as amateur production goes, single-camera coverage sometimes yields better results than multiple-camera coverage. Liberated from the problems of coordinating a crew, the director can concentrate on making that one camera render the most in-

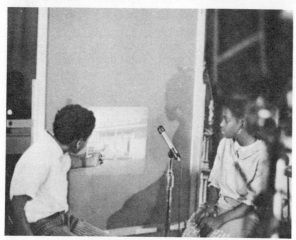

The portapak in full glory (top): snowy woods add realism to a junior high social studies playlet about The Swamp Fox *(shot taken off TV monitor).*

Rear projection to enliven single-camera coverage (bottom): note the projector on the left.

genious image possible. The "particular tricks" include:

Dollying the camera. A special kind of wheeled stand called a dolly permits you to move the camera through space while it is operating. In a financial pinch, you can improvise using a library cart, a children's wagon, or even a wheelchair.

Zooming and panning at the same time. When you can't come up with a dolly, this technique is the next best thing.

Rear projection. No camera movement here—the effect of "separate images" is achieved by projecting a movie or slide behind the actors onto a sheet or commercially-prepared rear projection material, such as Kodak's "Polycoat." In an instructional or news program, the performers might comment on the rear projected visuals. In fiction shows, the visuals can establish the setting.

Multiple-camera Coverage. Most TV studios and some portable systems have more than one camera. These cameras are capable of *simultaneous* operation, so that two or more subjects on a show (host and guest) can be covered without panning from one to the other, and the same subject can be covered through a variety of movie-like perspectives.

Most of the time, only one camera's shot is going out over the air or onto the videotape, although certain special effects, such as split-screen, blend two or more separate images. The director of the show spends his or her time in the control room 1) microphoning shot descriptions that the camera operators hear over their headsets, 2) observing the "on-air" shot on a TV set called the master monitor, and 3) fussing over when to cut from that shot to another camera's shot.

Cuts can reduce on-air camera movement. While Camera 1 is on the master monitor with a respectable mid-shot, Camera 2 might be executing a jerky dolly to an out-of-focus close-up. Once Camera 2's operator has settled down and focused, the director cuts from Camera 1 to Camera 2.

Switching

On a TV crew, the "switcher" (sometimes called the "technical director") is the person who punches the buttons and throws the levers which make the cuts, fades, and dissolves in a show. (The same name is given to the piece of machinery that makes the cuts, fades, and dissolves in a show.) It is his fingers which ultimately determine what ends up on the master monitor, although if the switcher and the director do not experience a meeting of minds, the director may send the switcher and his fingers home and punch the buttons himself.

Communication from director to switcher goes something like this:

"Fade to 1": The switcher pulls a lever which makes the picture being transmitted by Camera 1 go from dark to bright on the master monitor, like a fade-in in a movie.

"Cut to 2": The switcher punches from Camera 1 to Camera 2. On the master monitor, an effect appears that looks like a regular cut in a movie.

"Dissolve to 3": The switcher punches in Camera 3, but we don't see its picture on the master monitor until he pulls a lever which simultaneously fades down Camera 2's image and fades up Camera 3's image. This looks like a conventional movie dissolve.

"Fade to black": The switcher pulls a lever which makes the Camera 3 image gradually go dark on the master monitor, like a fade-out in a movie.

In large professional television studios, where videotape editing is now standard procedure and a show is typically covered by several complete "takes" and later edited, switching is not as vital to a program's success as it once was. But in small-studio production, switching is still the grammatical heart of the matter. In its ability to produce a cut to a close-up at the right moment, hide mistakes from the master monitor, and allow the director to alter props, sets, and actors without the audience thinking about it, switching in small-studio TV production is analogous to editing in filmmaking.

Here's a simple example. On Camera 1 we see kindly young Doc Jekyll downing his drug. Cut to Camera 2: a close-up of Jekyll's hand twitching. Offscreen, the make-up man charges in, dispensing liquid latex and crepe hair. This event is seen by Camera 1 but that doesn't matter because only Camera 2 is punched up on the master monitor. Cut to Camera 3: some test tubes bubbling up a storm. Meanwhile, the make-up man finishes and beats a hasty retreat. Cut back to Camera 1: Mr. Hyde snarls. Fade-out.

The switching-editing analogy breaks down eventually. A primary function of movie editing is to omit, not simply hide, portions of the action and, consequently, the time the omitted portions took to occur. This heightens pace and interest. Video-switching, on the other hand, serves only to present different viewpoints on an event as it happens continuously in time. It cannot shorten that event.

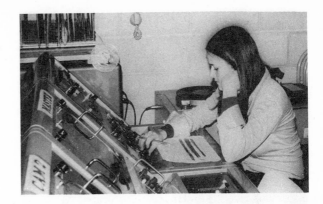

Television control room (top) and two-camera studio (center) in a junior high school.

Inside another school television facility (bottom), overlooking the studio floor from the control room.

Audio

In a typical studio television production, while the technical director is "mixing" images, the person in charge of audio is mixing sounds. The studio contains a variety of microphones which pick up the voices of the performers, as well as the commentary of off-camera announcers. Meanwhile, in the control room, sound effects and music can be added to the show from records and tapes.

While the director is calling out the camera and switching orders discussed above, he or she is also dispensing a set of correlated audio orders:

"Fade up the music": The audio engineer moves a potentiometer ("pot")—a rotating or sliding knob—which makes the music get gradually louder.

"Music under": The audio engineer lowers the volume of the music so it will be heard "underneath" the voices of the performers in the studio.

"Fade to chase theme": the audio engineer "dissolves" or "cross-fades" from the present music selection (say, a romantic piece coming off a tape recorder) to a second music selection (a chase theme cued up on the record player). If the first piece is not yet over, this makes for a smoother transition than an abrupt "flat cut."

In many TV shows, music and sound effects work the same way as in a radio play. Music can function as a "stinger" to the end of a scene, telling the audience in a few notes that something important has just occurred, or as a "bridge" to the next scene.

Sound effects can be used off-screen in television to evoke moods and images in the minds of the audience. (See Chapter 7 for sound effects production tips.) A crash of thunder, the patter of rain—perhaps combined with periodic dimming of the studio lights —and we are convinced a storm is raging outside the set. With a soundtrack that suggests enormous crowds and battles just beyond the borders of your TV screen, a modest production of *Julius Caesar* can be made to feel sweeping and spectacular. You could, of course, use a similar technique on the stage, with hidden speakers booming across the seats, but the effect would not be the same. The fundamental "openness" of the theater keeps the audience mindful that such sounds must be artificial. But the TV screen is "closed," and the thoughtful video director takes advantage of this.

Talent

Anyone who performs in front of a TV camera is called "the talent." This includes actors, announcers, acrobats, hosts, MC's, famous guests, anonymous guests, and newscasters. The label "talent" is not intended as an appraisal of the person in question, but if you watch UHF television commercials we don't need to tell you that.

Television acting occupies that rather expansive territory between stage acting and movie acting. Sometimes the TV actor gets to play his part, stage-like, in one unbroken recording of the entire script. But then parts of it may be recorded again, in film's piecemeal style, to give the videotape editor more options. Television make-up can be subtler than theatrical make-up, but not as subtle as for movies. Voice and gesture must be fairly "big" to come across on the low-fidelity TV screen, bigger than for film, but not nearly so big as on the stage.

To establish eye contact and grab the audience's attention, any talent in the role of commentator should stare directly into the camera. In multiple-camera shows, the talent sometimes has to keep an eye on the red "tally light" on top of each camera. Only the on-air camera has its tally illuminated. This also signals the camera operator whether his labor of the moment happens to be parading before the eyes of millions.

Activities

It's always a thrill for somebody when he sees himself on TV for the first time. Here's this box on which you're used to watching old movies and presidents and Lassie, and suddenly—bang!—there *you* are. For most people, kids included, this is a little discombobulating. You have to get used to the way you look on videotape, just as you have to get used to the way you sound on audiotape. But frequent feedback from television can actually enhance an individual's self-image and presence. Characteristics like a weak voice, a slouching posture, and an inability to finish sentences often disappear (on camera, at least) with practice.

Some educators believe that such potential benefits should be the explicit goal of using TV in the classroom. But for many children, unfocused feedback can be scary. In general, we feel it's best for personality changes to occur as a by-product of the kind of activity in which the student pitches a prepared bit to the camera.

The Variety Show

The variety show, combining comedy, juggling, dancing, singing, instrumental numbers, and other vaudeville acts, gives kids a chance to display their skills in the best possible light. If the crew is patient, the talent can do his stuff with the pressure turned way down. Unsure performers profit from videotape's built-in forgiveness. When a student blows a joke or hits a false note, the tape may be rewound for another go-round. A further bonus is that you don't have to get all the kids ready at the same time. A variety show on tape can be assembled over days or even weeks.

A must for student variety shows is "the blackout"—a short, punchy routine, usually funny, similar to the "skits" done around campfires. The word comes from vaudeville, presumably because the lights would black out as soon as the punch line was delivered. Blackout segments are a good way to engage all the elements of television—dialogue, props, lighting, coverage—without bogging down in the technical complexities of longer shows. Kids can even avoid memorizing lines by reading "idiot cards" (cue cards) held just off-camera. Sources for blackout ideas are: newspaper comic strips, joke books, school problems, TV commercials, and curriculum topics.

The Candid Camera Show

With the inevitability of rain on weekends, one of your students will want to try a candid camera show. The difficulty lies in thinking up situations which 1) won't get anybody into trouble, 2) are logistically possible within school schedules, 3) can be recorded with a hidden camera, and 4) are good. Beware lest this activity degenerate into the kids running around with a portapak, poking it at other kids who proceed to mug strenuously. That's not candor.

One stunt our students have used is to stop people on the street and try to *give* them spare change. In any group of four kids, one is usually willing to stick his neck (and his hand) out. An advantage of this exercise is that it does not rely on good sound recording. The fun comes in capturing the expressions on people's faces.

Once we placed the camera in the back seat of a parked car. Another time, the students did the bit in the lobby of their school. The camera operator hid behind some innocent-looking cardboard boxes that had been sitting around for several weeks.

Candid camera production is particularly useful in social studies, psychology, humanities, and other classes concerned with human behavior. Even if you do get mere mugging, it's fascinating to differentiate individual styles. As Colin Young puts it, "People do not behave naturally in front of the camera, but they do behave characteristically."

The Children's Show

Older kids can make TV shows for younger kids. Like our print activity called "The Children's Book," this format relieves the student from adult and peer judgments. Puppets work well for this kind

The candid camera show (top): giving away spare change.

The children's show (center): puppets are a natural subject.

The television interview (bottom): a portapak can go almost anywhere, even inside a wigwam.

The television documentary: high school students (top) tape an interview with Senator Edward Brooke for A Day in Congress. *John Clarke runs the portapak camera while Paul Cullen monitors the sound.*

Holding the portapak microphone (bottom), Bob O'Regan questions his senator.

of production. So does somebody with a winning personality who's able simply to face the camera and talk to kids, demonstrating the decimal point or the way to say "Good morning" in Hebrew or how to train a cat to shake hands.

Every student knows how some gadget works, and what you'll find if you take it apart. Television is a dandy medium for showing an audience the insides of a clock, a flashlight, a TV set, or any of the innumerable black boxes of our culture. In preparing their scripts, your student-instructors will probably pick up much useful knowledge themselves.

The best children's shows go beyond a simple stand-up lecture format. Usually there are several main characters, each with a distinct personality. Setting is important, too. In the past, kids have been transported to Mr. Wizard's workshop, Johnny Jupiter's grocery store, and Ding Dong School, more recently to Sesame Street and Misterogers' Neighborhood.

The Interview

Whatever you teach, there's bound to be someone in your community with information to share or with a possession that could enrich your curriculum—a pet lion, a set of rare books, a working model of *The Spirit of St. Louis*, a brilliant mind. If you have a studio and the subject is a good storyteller, there's nothing wrong with simply sitting her down under the lights and letting her talk. If you have a portable rig, though, consider the virtues of taping the subject on her own turf. In the interview illustrated on the previous page, for example, the portapak enabled an Algonquin Indian to demonstrate artifacts from inside a wigwam frame, instead of hauling them into a studio. (See Chapter 4 for practical tips on interviewing.)

Your more ambitious students may want to expand the simple interview into a Meet-the-Press type "panel show," or even into a full "television documentary." For example, we know a twelfth grader at Chelmsford High School in Massachusetts who decided to make a tape about his local congressman. Instead of simply interviewing the representative at home, the student raised $300 (through a bake sale and donations from the Elks and other civic groups) and followed him to Washington, D.C., accompanied by an interested teacher and two other students. The resulting TV program was called *A Day in Congress*.

The Sprocket-jockey Program

This format involves a "live" studio performer presenting a "canned" presentation on film. Sprocket jockeying goes back to television's earliest years, when Gabby Hayes used to interrupt some of Hollywood's worst westerns with comments and commercials. The practice reached its height in the late Fifties with out-of-work actors all over the country dressing up in bargain-basement monster suits to introduce, ridicule, and otherwise host old horror movies.

A student can take this approach with his school system's audio-visual aids. Instead of simply turning on a movie about red ants or a filmstrip about dangling participles, assign kids to jockey such materials down in the TV studio. Their job is to announce the item, tell us what to look for, and perhaps review it when finished. Stale lecturing is not needed. Like the harmless lunatics on *Creature Feature* and *Chiller Theater*, students can wear appropriate costumes and construct outlandish sets—anything to put the viewers in a lively, happy mood.

The Television Play

Inside a TV studio, or even just in front of a portapak, the traditional "class play" takes on new dimensions. Again, keep in mind Chapter 1's argument that media do not replace each other. If the stage has struck you and your students, by all means stay on the stage. But theatrical dramas and comedies do lend themselves excitingly to television.

Consider *Hamlet* with the soliloquies done voice-over while Hamlet paces about, or with the gravedigger scene taped in your local cemetary. You can do *Our Town* in and around *your* town. Musical comedy works especially well. For a big, professional sound, kids can "mouth" songs from commercial records and tapes.

Every school subject has a history. Important moments in the evolution of astronomy, dictionaries, and numbers can all be adapted as television plays and staged for the camera. The library research required for a credible script means much legitimate learning, and the performance and playback help make the knowledge stick.

Standards

As the newest member of the media family, television inspires a kind of awe in even the most sophisticated user. The simple fact that you can take a portapak into a classroom, out on a boat, or up in an airplane and come back with good-quality, moving, instantly replayable images with sound will astound almost anyone for whom you perform the service. But as the novelty pales, your audience is going to expect (and deserve) more complex productions. Quite appropriately, they'll judge your efforts according to standards inspired by professional TV,

The television play: ninth graders adapted Poe's Masque of the Red Death *for the video screen. Post-production electronic editing enabled the students to alternate outdoor portapak scenes of funerals (top) and nocturnal visitations (center) with an indoor studio scene of Death invading the masque (bottom).*

which is why you'll want to avoid the following common mistakes.

Visual Incoherence. Several years ago, one of the authors took a group of second graders to the zoo with a portapak. We had a nice time and the tape turned out all right, but it had some problems. For one thing, the kid behind the camera forgot to keep it pointed at what the kid with the microphone was talking about. Conversely, the kid with the microphone did not worry too much about whether the camera was shooting anything that related to his commentary, or, indeed, whether the tape was even rolling. So we ended up with lots of ducks on the screen while interviews with goats proceeded on the soundtrack.

Just as irritating were all the shots that managed to be either unsteady or out of focus or both. The panacea for unsteadiness is simple: use a tripod. Alternatively, practice the art of hand-holding the camera rigidly. Focus is a stickier problem. The typical television camera is fitted out with a zoom lens whose "focusing ring" allows you to set an exact camera-subject distance on a scale of feet and meters. You don't need to measure this distance because the camera's viewfinder reveals focus errors as well as framing errors. When the lens is zoomed out all the way to "wide-angle," the image contains so much depth of field that the focusing can be imprecise. However, as soon as you zoom in, the depth of field narrows dramatically, and the subject will go out of focus unless the camera-subject distance has been accurately set on the lens. The professional solution—and most kids above fourth grade can master it—is to zoom in all the way on the subject, focus, zoom out, and *then* start the tape rolling. You are now free to zoom in and out on the subject, provided its distance from the camera does not change.

Visual Monotony. A news show does not have to consist of just a commentator's face. That's dull. Much of his material can be done "voice-over"—over charts, over maps, over drawings, over photographs, over movies, over slides, over newspaper headlines. All of these materials show up well on the TV screen.

In a multiple-camera studio, switching from an announcer to a picture is the most basic of procedures. The kind of switcher known as a "special effects generator" even permits you to combine announcer and visual in a single image—say, the visual "behind" the announcer (via the generator's "matte and key" capability) or the announcer added "over" the visual in one quadrant of the screen (via the generator's "wipe" capability).

As we mentioned in the Concepts section, such images can be simulated in a one-camera studio, either by simply zooming in on a graphics display or by rear-projecting slides and movies. The trick in rear-projection is to light the announcer from the side, using a piece of heavy cardboard to throw a shadow across the screen and keep the image from washing out.

Aural Incoherence. The believability of a dramatic show is heightened considerably by keeping the microphones out of camera range. Unfortunately, you then have to bend over backwards to get good sound, since the further a mike is from its subject, the more the sound will be overwhelmed by the ambience of your studio or location. TV audiences are appreciably less tolerant of incoherent audio than incoherent video. So:

1. Buy good microphones, not the $15.00 variety most schools get for their portapaks. Let your ear shop. (Sony's ECM-21, for example, which costs about $50.00, will increase the coherence of your portapak shows a hundred percent.)
2. Use unidirectional or cardioid (semi-directional) mikes rather than omni-directional ones.

There is almost no such thing as speaking too loudly in an amateur video production.

As the label implies, omni-directional mikes pick up sound in all directions, thus increasing echo and ambience. They have their day when a round-table discussion must be recorded with a single microphone.

3. Get the mike as close to the subject as possible. For interviews and talk shows, consider lavalier mikes, the kind that hang around the talent's neck or pin to his clothing. With some ingenuity and a piece of string, you can jerry-build a lavalier mike.
4. Do not let anyone step on, finger, or fiddle with the mike cord while the tape is rolling unless you want a thunderstorm on your soundtrack. If your mike has a thin cable, replace it with a heavier, better-shielded one.
5. At every opportunity, urge the talent to speak up, articulate, project. Even under ideal recording conditions, you will get poor sound if the talent mumbles. There is almost no such thing as speaking too loudly in amateur video production. The TV screen and speaker have a way of toning down flamboyant performances and making them seem right.

Undefined Subjects. Amateur portapak work is commonly awash with the pointless congestion of "multi-subject" shots—wide-angle views of streets full of cars or rooms jammed to the walls with people talking. The other symptom of the portapak operator who can't define his or her subject is coverage through a succession of rapid bursts of tape instead of long, continuous, revealing runs.

Inappropriate Subjects. Television is an audio-visual medium. It works best when the subject moves and makes sounds. A visit to the town dump is not likely to be very engaging on videotape if all you end up with are pans across silent bottles and zooms into inanimate cans. (These same "still" subjects might make a terrific slide-tape or photo exhibit.) But if you work a bit of noisy action into the program—a seagull scavaging or a man sorting the bottles or a machine crushing the cans—you may have something. At the same time, given the limited editing possibilities of half-inch videotape, you don't want to attempt an idea that's *too* dynamic. The eighth grade war movie analyzed in Chapter 8, with its miniature castles and fights on trains and D. W. Griffith inter-cutting, would have been impossible with a portapak.

Cuing Errors. A mistake that commonly plagues the talent side of in-school television is the "jumped cue." In a videotaped production, there is absolutely no poetry in an actor starting his bit before the tape is rolling, the camera is faded up, the mike is opened, and the background music is faded down. The talent should always wait for the "cue" to begin. (In studio production, the floor manager points at him.)

The opposite problem is also familiar. Fade up on Jimmy Brown. Nothing happens. Uncomfortable, Jimmy stares into the camera. Nothing happens some more. Finally, Jim gets it into his head that he should perhaps begin to think about saying his first line. Intuitively, the audience senses that they are in the hands of nonprofessionals. This problem is referred to as "missing your cue" or "not picking up your cue."

Flatness. The theater stage is a set of flat boards lying at right angles to a set of flat walls. The video stage is all the world. Classroom TV productions often suffer from lack of depth—everything happens on the same "base line," parallel to the camera's plane of vision. If care is taken to catch the sound, actors can be highly mobile, walking toward or away from the camera. The camera itself can be moved through space on a dolly, an effect which communicates a greater sense of the third dimension than mere zooming. Camera angle is also an important variable. Not all your set-ups need to be at eye level.

Bewitched Switching. Confronted with a multiple-camera studio for the first time, many students switch capriciously. They go to Camera 2 before it has a good shot (or a shot that is appreciably different from Camera 1's) and they dissolve (because it looks neat) where a straight cut would be more appropriate. Such techcentricity should be discouraged.

Pack Ratting. It's bewildering how many educators believe that as long as a TV camera gets pointed at a school assembly, a Thanksgiving pageant, or a guest speaker, a worthwhile recording will result. But conservation is not always a virtue; some events are of the moment. We have seen shelves of tapes nobody wants to watch taking up valuable space in a small studio. So when someone asks the ominous question media teachers hear so often—"Could we get a videotape of it?"—your first line of defense should be another question—"Who's going to look at it?"

Timidity. This is the subtlest classroom video pitfall. We have seen a student-made interview program in which, had the director taken the initiative to move the subject around a little, that subject would not have been washed out by the light of a background window. We have seen a videotaped concert in which, had the camera operator summoned the gumption to climb up to the catwalks, he could have picked up a wealth of fascinating particulars—the face of the conductor, the scores of the various instruments, the hands of the musicians, the reactions of the audience. We have seen a school-studio mystery play in which, had somebody agitated to disconnect the overhead lights and fix them below eye level, the atmosphere would have instantly thickened with a proper measure of gloom.

Certain documentary subjects, of course, cannot or should not be manipulated by the TV director. But on the whole, don't hesitate to push all elements of the medium around. Your eyes will thank you for it when, years from now, you decide to watch the tape again.

Television is the prime example of a once-imagined future come to pass, a future that, taken into our own hands, seems no more apocalyptic than aesthetic. On the horizon, the medium of the next future looms, waiting to knock us silly and then to be endowed with the standards that will enable it to tell stories, document events, create moods, record the delicacies of human spirit, and do all the other things that make a medium worth having around. Already we can witness crude experiments with this vehicle, imagine its potential, and begin to get its name right —*holography.*

1. *Radio in Elementary Education* by Roy Willey and Helen Young (Boston: D. C. Heath and Company, 1948) is out of print, and likely to remain so.

2. The bible of studio-television is still Gerald Millerson's *The Technique of Television Production* (New York: Hastings House, 1968).

3. A particularly informative account of the portable (non-studio) television revolution is found in *Peterson's Guide to Video Tape Recording*, a magazine-format book published by Peterson Publishing Company, 8490 Sunset Boulevard, Los Angeles, CA 90069.

Media and people 10

The more likely a student is to use what he has learned in school, the less likely the school is to care. Project-oriented courses in art, drama, wood shop, music, photography, and home economics rarely cop the prestige reserved for English, math, history, and other "major" subjects. And yet, more of us solve problems in our daily lives by hammering nails and drawing diagrams than we do by knowing Boyle's Law or the six (or was it seven?) causes of the War of 1812.

In recent years, education critics have begun some tough probing of academics in the public schools. Not only are these critics questioning the *value* of learning the traditional disciplines, they are also questioning *whether* anyone is learning them in the first place. Do students remember anything about higher mathematics, two years or even two months after Calculus I? Do they remember the content of the final exam, or do they just remember taking it? Do they learn German in their German classes, or do they just learn how many years they "had" it?

Think back on your own schooling a moment. We'll wager that your most immediate and gratifying memories include those times when classroom learning became synonymous with creative production. Perhaps you recall having your poem published in the school paper, or your science project about robots, or your extra-credit series of Latin cartoons, or the time you reported on Robert Oppenheimer by role-playing him in conversation with Albert Einstein. We'll also wager that your nonexistent memo-

ries include those times you were lectured on the difference between mitosis and meiosis or read about the workings of the coordinating conjunctive.

Our own response to the disparity between what is taught and what is learned is not radical. We feel it *is* important for everyone to have a handle on biology, chemistry, physics, mathematics, history, grammar, literature, and at least one foreign culture, including its language. But we also feel it's important to put this commitment in perspective, to understand that when students study simply by memorizing data, they seem to take very little away with them, but when they study concretely and actively, they seem to care about, remember, and reapply the experience.

The marriage of real-world media production and school-world subjects really has two potential payoffs. First, the student masters enough of the *curriculum* that, once out of school, he is able to sort out the world with something of the scientist's eye, the mathematician's mind, the historian's perspective, the writer's sensibility. Second, the student masters enough *media production knowhow* that, once out of school, he is able to use media tools for a wide range of personal goals, both practical and aesthetic.

Every community has its share of adults who regard "active production" and "multi-media" and "creativity" not as the exclusive domain of elite professionals, but as something they can, and must, experience first hand. Creativity for them is a basic

All the activities discussed in this book can become occasions for genuine creativity in the home.

human instinct. They meet its demands head on, without capitulating to questions like "Is it worth the time?" or "Shouldn't I have a mass audience first?"

All the activities discussed in this book can become occasions for genuine creativity in the home. We know families who use the medium of *stage* in putting on puppet plays, backyard circuses, magic acts, and Christmas pageants for themselves and their neighbors. *Design* is also apt for holidays and other special events, for it is the medium of greeting cards and home decorations. Dress-making, poster-making, game-making, model-making, comic-book-making—these are all design activities that fit comfortably into the daily routine.

We generally think of *print* as something worth doing only when we're going to be published professionally, yet lots of people write poems, letters, stories, skits, brain teasers, and humorous essays solely for the amusement of their friends or nephews or selves.

Photography has been around the average home for many years. With the help of a tape recorder and a record player, the obligatory "slide show" can be turned into something remarkable—a good amateur slide-tape. With a small but enthusiastic investment of time and effort, the family's 8mm camera, tape recorder, and (soon) portable TV camera can cease being mere novelties and start helping members become makers of *movies, radio*, and *television*.

Beyond the home movie, home radio show, home vaudeville routine, or home poster is the amateur media production which attempts to connect with people on a professional level. For example, one of the authors recently saw a slide-tape by a Canadian National Park ranger. The producer combined his best nature shots with symphonic music and personal, poetic commentary on a dimension of the park most tourists never experience—the coming of winter, when animals can travel down from the Rockies to find food and humans can travel up from the towns to find solitude. In this format, the ranger's message carried an impact and a conviction he probably couldn't have achieved simply by lectur-

ing. He was clearly proud of his effort, and began scheduling showings of the slide-tape not just to his immediate circle of friends, but to all interested park visitors.

Our second example is a "home book" called *Brain Child*. Its author, a New York woman named Peggy Napear, spent the years from 1964 to 1972 administering the controversial Doman-Delacato treatment for neurological dysorganization to her mentally retarded daughter, Jane. The diary she kept during this period proved so engrossing, hopeful, and moving that Harper & Row decided to publish it verbatim, even though the author had never written anything of this magnitude before and her style lacked professional polish.

These are just two examples among many. The point is that media are there to serve us, and rare is the individual who cannot find a meaningful use for some of them in his life. It's simply a matter of overcoming the intimidations and biases of contemporary culture.

The mystique of media, discussed in the Introductory Essay, is powerful indeed. At its worst, it actually causes some people to underestimate their capacity for creative output. One symptom is the attitude that before you can become a media user you must first enroll in a university with a "communications" or "visual studies" department or, at the very least, take adult-education "media" courses.

Yet other people, children especially, take it for granted that media are to be used, not worshipped. They are not hung up on media. They don't "do media." They do messages.

In every school kids are growing up putting on plays, writing stories, making magazines, publishing newspapers, and drawing cartoons. And in every school with the necessary resources, kids are growing up producing their own TV shows, radio dramas, and movies.

There is magic in the ability of the average child to pick up a clunky hand puppet and turn it into a character, giving it an existence apart from his own. There is no magic in the puppet; the magic is in the child. There is no magic in film, radio, or television either; the magic is in the kids and adults who make these forms work.

True, media use will not solve the deepest problems of anyone's life. Playing charades does not lead to brotherhood. Community sings do not build communities. Home movies will not head off divorce.

But in our rush to cut to the causes of personal and social ills, we may miss the glorious little moments that people in any time and place—at school, at home, at work, in a church, in a hospital, on a vacation—can produce when they use cameras, microphones, pencils, puppets, gestures, and voices. The creativity drive is one of the few sides of human nature that makes us feel right about ourselves. The art in each of us is worth the struggle.

Sources and Resources

Although it avoids technological formats, we recommend the series called *The Family Creative Workshop*. These books outline such "home media" projects as bookbinding, ceramics, stained glass, carving, and toy-making. They are available through Time-Life Books, Time and Life Building, Chicago, IL 60611.

Appendix

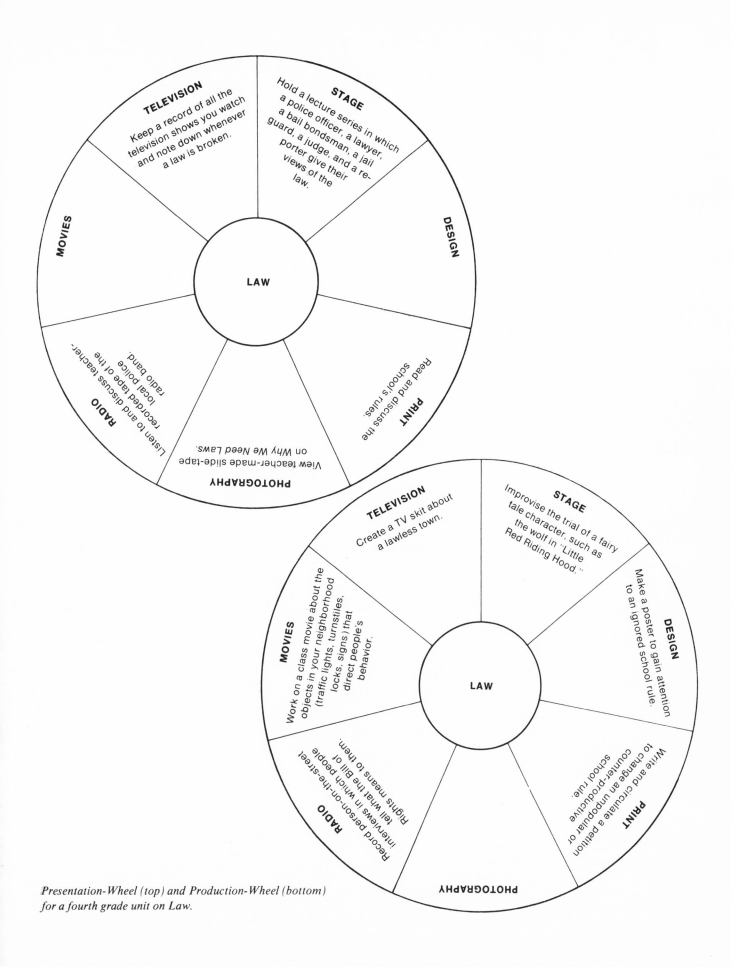

Presentation-Wheel (top) and Production-Wheel (bottom)
for a fourth grade unit on Law.

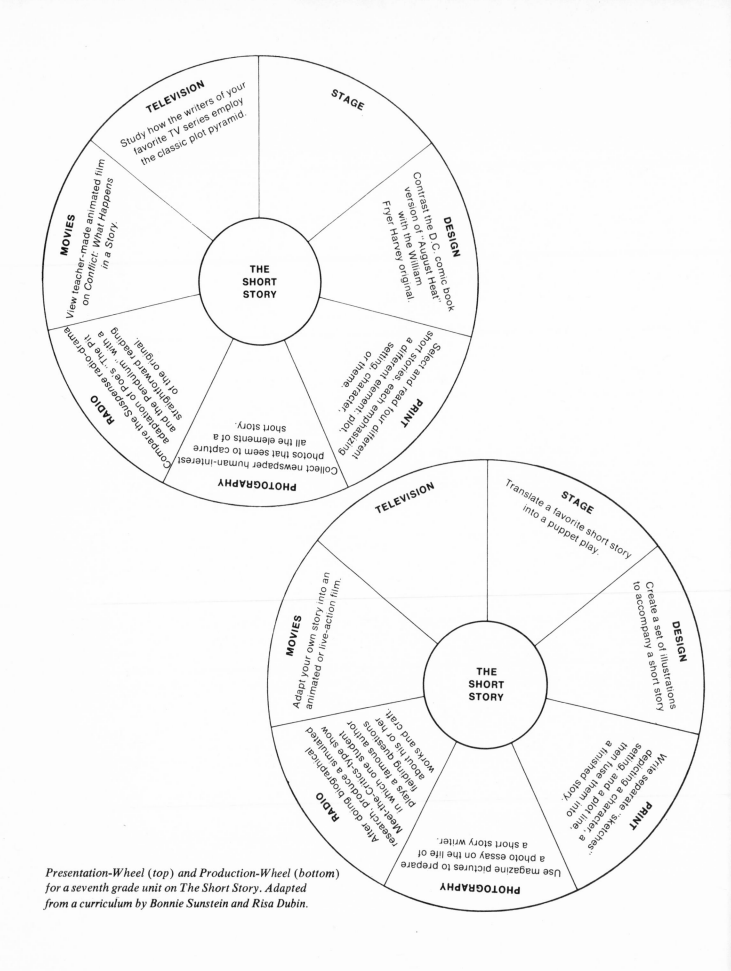

Presentation-Wheel (top) and Production-Wheel (bottom) for a seventh grade unit on The Short Story. Adapted from a curriculum by Bonnie Sunstein and Risa Dubin.

Presentation-Wheel (top):

THE SHORT STORY

STAGE

DESIGN — Contrast the D.C. comic book version of "August Heat" with the William Fryer Harvey original.

PRINT — Select and read four different short stories, each emphasizing a different element: plot, setting, character, or theme.

PHOTOGRAPHY — Collect newspaper human-interest photos that seem to capture all the elements of a short story.

RADIO — Compare the Suspense radio-drama adaptation of Poe's "The Pit and the Pendulum" with a straightforward reading of the original.

MOVIES — View teacher-made animated film on *Conflict: What Happens in a Story.*

TELEVISION — Study how the writers of your favorite TV series employ the classic plot pyramid.

Production-Wheel (bottom):

THE SHORT STORY

STAGE — Translate a favorite short story into a puppet play.

DESIGN — Create a set of illustrations to accompany a short story.

PRINT — Write separate "sketches": a character, a setting, and a plot line; then fuse them into a finished story.

PHOTOGRAPHY — Use magazine pictures to prepare a photo essay on the life of a short story writer.

RADIO — After doing biographical research, produce a simulated Meet-the-Critics-type show in which one student plays a famous author fielding questions about his or her works and craft.

MOVIES — Adapt your own story into an animated or live-action film.

TELEVISION

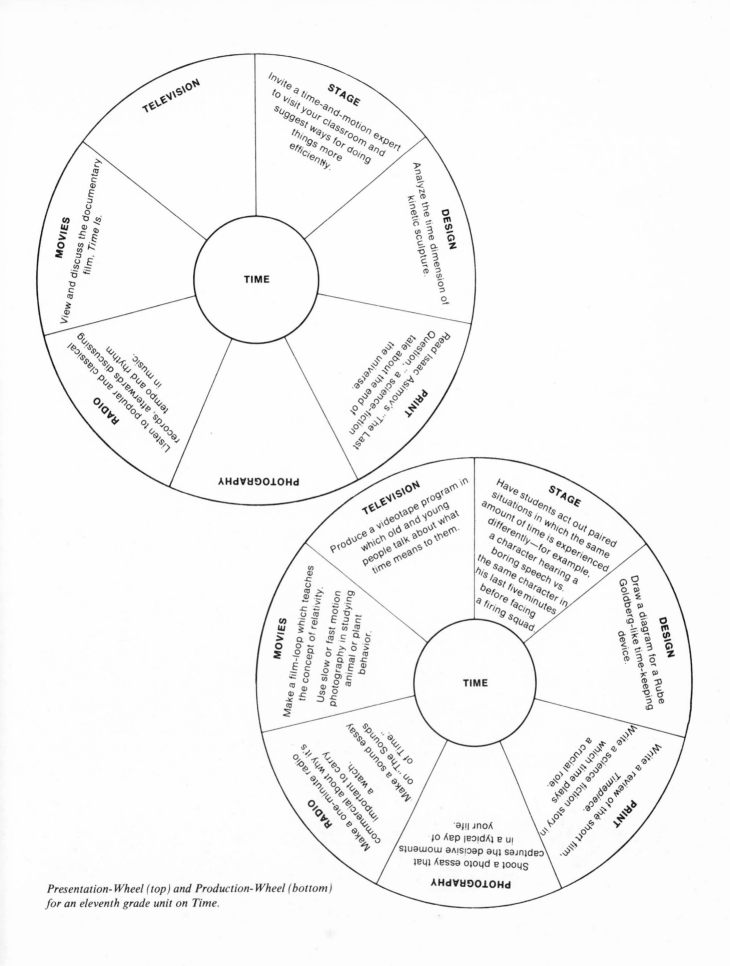

*Presentation-Wheel (top) and Production-Wheel (bottom)
for an eleventh grade unit on Time.*

Index